Cecilia Sala is a journalist, war correspondent, and podcaster. Her reporting has appeared in *L'Espresso*, *Vanity Fair*, and *Wired*. She has covered crises in Venezuela, protests in Chile, and Iran, the fall of Kabul to the Taliban in August 2021, and the war in Ukraine. On December 19, 2024, she was arrested in Tehran by the Iranian regime and held in solitary confinement in the Evin Prison, where she remained for three weeks before being released. Soon after been freed, she returned to reporting from the field, continuing to cover global conflicts and political upheavals.

Oonagh Stransky has been a translator of Italian literature for over twenty years. Some of the writers whose work she has brought into English include Pier Paolo Pasolini, Carlo Lucarelli, Giuseppe Pontiggia, and Roberto Saviano. Her translation of Domenico Starnone's *The House on Via Gemito* was shortlisted for the Oxford-Weidenfeld Translation Prize and for the American Literary Translators Association 2024 Italian Prose in Translation Award. She currently lives in Italy.

THE FIRE

Cecilia Sala

THE FIRE

VOICES OF A GENERATION IN IRAN, UKRAINE, AND AFGHANISTAN

Translated from the Italian
by Oonagh Stransky

Europa Editions
27 Union Square West, Suite 302
New York NY 10003
www.europaeditions.com
info@europaeditions.com

First publication 2025 by Europa Editions

Translation by Oonagh Stransky
Original title: *L'incendio. Reportage su una generazione tra Iran, Ucraina e Afghanistan*

Library of Congress Cataloging in Publication Data is available
ISBN 979-8-88966-150-4

Sala, Cecilia
The Fire

Cover design and illustration by Ginevra Rapisardi

Prepress by Grafica Punto Print – Rome

Printed in Canada

CONTENTS

For Kamila and Maryam

THE FIRE

Where this Book Begins

In January, the wind that blows through Qom is frenzied, electric, and impossible to avoid. Neither the wide avenues nor the houses, built low so as not to cast shadows on the minarets, offer any protection. Sand blows directly into your face and eyes. Down the street, you see dark shapes moving in a strange dance: chadors, the women within kicking their feet and waving their arms so that no part of their bodies is ever exposed to air.

Qom is the holy city of the Islamic Republic of Iran. It was here, in January 2020, in the great blue-domed mosque, that the funeral ceremony of General Qasem Soleimani took place before his body was laid to rest in the cemetery of Kerman, his native village in the middle of the desert.

Soleimani was the commander of the Islamic Revolutionary Guards Quds Force, the special corps that decides Iran's foreign policy within the region and implements missions beyond its borders, in the Middle East and farther afield. Much more charismatic than contemporary ayatollahs, his face was everywhere: on posters in the bedrooms of teenagers from conservative families, and on stickers plastered to their scooters. Even the community play room in Qom—where a stuffed toy resembling Donald Trump sits in the center of the room, for children to kick or throw balls at—was renamed after the general. There's even a popular spy show on television that everyone knows was inspired by Soleimani.

Before his death, there were rumors in Tehran that he might

run for president, with the elections slated for June 18, 2021. He would surely win, they said. Instead, Soleimani and his bodyguards were killed by an American drone, an MQ-9 Reaper, at the Baghdad airport on January 3, 2020.

I traveled to Tehran to gauge how Iranians felt about his death. My friend Nasim—a professor who does not believe in God, grows grapes in his garden to get round the alcohol ban, and who will eventually take part in the protests after the death of Mahsa Amini—put it clearly: "Soleimani was a terrorist. So were the people who killed him." Nasim frequently hosts parties for friends at his house with the garden, eager to share his homemade Shiraz, which he stores in plastic bottles, smoke opium in Afghan pipes, and listen to music. On the evening I was there, *Amour censure* played over and over. A raw and beautiful song, I had never heard it before, but it ended up keeping me company (in my headphones) for months to come. That was the last party I went to for a very long time.

During the pandemic, Qom was the second largest global epicenter of Covid after Wuhan. People with lung infections died while waiting to be admitted to hospitals due to a lack of beds. Millions of people, Iranians and Iraqis alike, attended Soleimani's funeral; it was so crowded that fifty people were trampled to death and around two hundred were wounded. That ceremony was almost certainly an immense hotspot for the virus.

I flew back to Italy from Qom on one of the few direct flights that still link us to Iran. When I landed in Milan, people were just starting to talk about Codogno and Vo' Euganeo, two towns that would soon become known all over the world for being the first Covid hotspots outside China.

Some days later, I went with my family to a restaurant in Rome to celebrate my mother's birthday. After dessert, the manager, who knew us well, let me smoke at the table. We were the only ones there anyway, he pointed out. Later that same night, Italian Prime Minister Giuseppe Conte gave a press conference in which he announced the first national curfew in Italy since the fall of Benito Mussolini.

For the following two years, work—which is to say, travel—was practically impossible, not to mention going to a party. The first time I danced again, after being at Nasim's, was in Kyiv, on a bitterly cold night, the thermometer registering temperatures of negative six degrees Celsius, at the end of January 2022. Just three weeks before the country was invaded.

This book brings together encounters, historic events, and conversations that took place in Iran, Ukraine, and Afghanistan, where the chief protagonist is one specific generation.

Young people in their twenties in Iran—whom the Iranian Revolutionary Guards and the ayatollah's media agencies consider a "lost generation," with whom they no longer know how to communicate—ignited a protest the likes of which has not been seen since the Revolution that toppled the monarchy in 1979.

When twenty-year-olds in today's Afghanistan were born, the Taliban had recently been chased out; in 2021, these young people witnessed the return of the militia. They grew up imagining—and then building—their lives around premises that are incompatible with Taliban principles. They're the ones who have paid most heavily for the way we abandoned them, an action that has had significant consequences beyond Afghanistan's borders, which we initially ignored, and which later harmed us.

The war in Ukraine is being fought by its young people. Ukrainian twenty-year-olds were the key players in the last successful European revolution, that of 2014. They were punished for that in 2022 with Vladimir Putin's full-scale invasion; now those same young men and women are fighting again.

This book examines the three fires that are currently raging across the globe and the generation that is growing up amid the flames.

Part One:
Iran

I.
Being Twenty in Tehran

It's June in Tehran. The soles of your shoes stick to the pavement, you sweat in your hijab, with its long sleeves and cape that conceals your body down to your ankles. The path you take through the city follows the shade of the *ficus sycamorus*, a somewhat larger and more majestic species of fig tree—the few that are left, anyway, after the city started chopping them down to make room for cars. That summer, in some parts of Iran, the temperatures reached fifty-six degrees Celsius.

"Have they forgotten that half the population has to walk around bundled up, and all because they decided it should be that way? Are the men in the government trying to kill us women?" Sadira rolls a cigarette while walking down the busy sidewalk.[1] It's crowded with people and policemen. A woman who smokes always has to look over her shoulder to check for white vans with a green stripe—the Gasht-e Ershad, or morality police—before digging into her purse or pocket for a lighter. "All clear. Let's just cross that intersection," she says. We're standing near a bank where there are surveillance cameras.

Sadira speaks four languages and is trying to find a job that will allow her to work in an embassy abroad. She has already had two interviews, and they both went well. Even though she detests the government, she's willing to work for them as long as she does not have to live in a society with "grim and absurd" rules and can stay in touch with her family, because "I don't want to abandon my country entirely." She knows perfectly well that as soon as she left her interview at the Ministry of Foreign

Affairs, the first thing her potential future employers did was scrutinize her social media profiles. Her Instagram account is the same as it always was; she hasn't deleted any of the photos that show her without a veil, and her stories, as of September 2022, are an uninterrupted flow of songs and tributes to the *Jin, Jiyan, Azadi* (Woman, Life, Freedom) movement.

On September 20, 2022, Sadira wrote to me: "The world is a violent place. How can you Europeans pretend not to know this? How have you forgotten this fact? There's life on this planet! People and regimes are living things. We're not museum pieces, like you are. And we never will be, thank you very much."

That date marks the beginning of a protest that went on to pose the greatest threat to the Iranian institutions since the one that successfully brought down the monarchy and led to the Islamic Revolution of 1979.

I talk to another woman, Forouzan, by video chat; she is in a public park in the Chitgar neighborhood in western Tehran. "In this part of town, you have to go out of your way to find a girl wearing a hijab. And here, when men see you on the street without a veil, they give you a fist bump," she says. Forouzan is twenty-three years old and studying electronics at university. She has short curly hair, round glasses, and is wearing a black bomber jacket. She's been part of the movement since day one, or earlier, since September 16, the day Mahsa Amini died in the hospital and a photograph of her, intubated and covered in bruises, started circulating on the web, first in Iran and then around the world. There were no marches or protests that day, but a group that Forouzan and Assim, her best friend, belonged to started graffitiing Mahsa's name in bathrooms on campus and on subway cars. "We had no idea what we were starting."

Forouzan has never worn a hijab: she wears her hair short and her closet is full of androgynous clothes. Dressing in a more masculine way always seemed to her like the best way of avoiding trouble with the morality police. But after September 16, the white vans with the green stripe pretty much disappeared from the streets. "People feel less afraid of breaking the rules now."

The park that Forouzan calls me from has a skatepark set in the middle of an orchard, crowded with young women. Recent photos of city parks, subway escalators, bazaars, malls, and people on their way to work or out shopping show hardly any women wearing veils—mind-blowing to anyone who knew what life was like in Tehran only a few months earlier. This is a powerful but fragile new world. "How can things ever go back after this?"

These women are not the ones who went out and protested. These women didn't have the courage to fight the armed members of the Basij, they weren't willing to risk losing an eye after getting shot in the face with a rubber bullet or to get arrested. But they were courageous enough to go outside dressed however they wanted in early 2023.[2]

"All together, we managed to create a new normal. It happened spontaneously. Now comes the hard part: protecting it."

Before the wave of protests, signs of micro-rebellion were everywhere. Each time I took a Turkish Airlines or Qatar Airways flight home from Iran, I saw women remove their hijabs immediately after take-off. I'd study the men sitting next to them; their expressions were always of complicity.

From Yazd to Isfahan, it's normal to see women with nose jobs, barely bothering with headscarves, their long hair dyed blue, green, platinum or purple tumbling down their almost entirely exposed shoulders, with fake long nails, artificially enhanced cheekbones, tattooed eyebrows, and dressed in skinny jeans. Twenty-year-olds use VPN services—the virtual networks that allow them to hide from geolocation systems—to break through censorship walls and get their daily fill of social media, with the authorities and their families well aware of it.

Once, one summer, I went to a restaurant located at the foot of the ski slopes to the north of Tehran with some friends. It was a weekday, and the place was half-empty. I felt embarrassed because I was the only one wearing a veil. At the only other table in the place, all the women had taken their headscarves off as soon as they sat down. On weekends, if you go out for breakfast to one of the cafés in the center of the capital city, you regularly see groups of young people gobbling up *nan-e* flatbread, carrot jam, and Persian omelets to help them get over their hangovers. It's also hard to miss their dilated pupils, from the ecstasy they took the night before.

Tehran parties are renowned. An uncorroborated legend has it that all the bootleggers who sell alcohol needed for cocktails are employees of the Russian embassy. Drugs are easier to find than gin. "I have enough amphetamines to fight three wars and then die of a heart attack," Dilsad, a young Kurdish man, boasted to me in November 2022.

Back then, the most intense protests took place in Iranian Kurdistan. In Mahabad, Sardasht, Piranshahir, and Oshnavieh, there was serious talk of how to obtain weapons because "there can't be a revolution without them." Dilsad had tried to obtain rifles and ammunition from the Kurds in Iraq who live only a few kilometers away, on the other side of the mountains that mark the northwest border. "I went there, too. I learned how to fight on that steep and rugged terrain. I came back home with advice from our Iraqi brothers, but none of their Kalashnikovs."

Once, at a party in Tehran, I met a Kurdish girl, a friend of Dilsad's, who had learned Italian because she was passionate about lyrical opera. She was a frustrated soprano: in Iran, women are not allowed to sing solo parts in public, they can't record their voices or sell their music. They can only sing in choirs as accompaniment to male singers. Iranian twenty-year-olds have joined forces with a number of club owners to find remote places for their raves, they have a clandestine—though not perfectly concealed—network that they use for parties. They mainly play electronic music, but occasionally they use the locales for lyrical concerts and opera performances to help out people like Dilsad's friend, and all the other frustrated sopranos in Iran.

The Best, the Excluded

Almost two-thirds of all university students in Iran are female. Among those who protested in the name of Mahsa Amini were aspiring diplomats, like Sadira, as well as aeronautical engineers and physicists. Iran needs its brains and, in some professions, it is even willing to ignore the no-longer-silent rebellions of its employees to keep functioning. A double standard applies: if I cross paths with you while you're working for your country and you're doing your job, then it's fine because you're a necessary cog in the wheel, but if I see you out in the street and you're protesting and questioning the order of things, then you become an enemy because you threaten my existence and you deserve a violent punishment. Students and young employees in Iran spend the best years of their lives living between these two extremes.

Assim meets up with Forouzan in the skatepark in Chitgar. Assim is the son of a famous university professor and will soon graduate in aeronautical engineering. The Islamic Revolutionary Guard monitors that department and its best students very carefully. In fact, Assim has already been selected, essentially without being asked, for an experimental Air Force program focused on missiles, a pet project of General Amir Ali Hajizadeh himself, who has commanded the Air Force of the Revolutionary Guards since 2009. "But," Assim says, "I'd rather flee the country than spend my time dropping bombs on gigantic models of Israeli military sites."

Assim is passionate about aeronautics in the private sector and was enthusiastic when, at the beginnings of the protests, one of his heroes, Elon Musk, said that he would help the Iranian protesters get around digital repression by sending them hundreds of Starlink satellites—the tools produced by SpaceX that allow people to stay connected to the internet despite any perturbations, whatever the circumstances. Four months later, Assim feels let down. "Something clearly went wrong, it didn't work. The devices are here in Iran, but we haven't seen them."

While we're talking, the minister of Telecommunications, Eisa Zarepour, makes a cryptic announcement: she confirms that the Starlink satellites have arrived in the country, but her message relays no concern whatsoever. "We welcome the technology, as long as it is used according to our laws." Meanwhile, SpaceX releases its own scant announcement to say that the thousand or so devices have arrived, but they don't mention the protests at all. "They tricked us," Assim says flatly.

When Forouzan introduced Assim to me, she said he goes to "the genius factory," a nickname for Sharif University of Technology in Tehran. Located in the center of the city, the campus is a network of buildings and laboratories that extend from Azadi Avenue—where *Azadi* means Freedom, as in the rallying cry heard in the square—to the busy three-lane Yadegaran Expressway, named after the memorial to the Republic. Sharif is an exceptional university, and the students who graduate from it will carry its name with them throughout their lives. It has come to stand for a person who is brilliant and independent; someone who is studying (or has studied) a highly complicated subject, and who earns (or will earn) very well. I know two women who received their doctorates from Sharif University, and one of them works as an executive for a major Texan oil company, and the other has a leadership position in one of the world's most important tech companies. Only two years after finishing their studies, both were earning nearly two hundred thousand dollars a year.

The "genius factory" in Tehran may not have the means or

laboratories of MIT, but it is the MIT of the Middle East. The polytechnic is a leader in a different way. In Iran, the majority of students of STEM subjects are women. In the United States, men make up over 60% of students in science, technology, engineering, and math. Globally, 65% of STEM students are male. In this, the Republic of Islam is an important exception.

Iran produces more highly skilled graduates than its fossilized economy can absorb. The government hires a portion of them and gives them tasks that are often very different from what they dreamed they would one day do, but, with a withering GDP year after year, new jobs are hard to come by. The exclusion of young people from the country's traditional economy has created a mass of people who do not depend on the government for a salary to pay their rent. In fact, the young people out protesting are those who, in the past few years, have managed to separate their professional lives from the economy of the regime. They had no other choice: there was no room for them in the closely woven fabric created by pseudo-private foundations run by clerics and the Revolutionary Guards. Essentially, the economy of Iran is an oligarchy in the hands of the mullahs and the Guards, and the city where this is most evident is Mashhad, located in the east towards the border with Turkmenistan and Afghanistan. Nicknamed "the hidden capital," it is the birthplace of most of Iran's leaders. Supreme Leader Ali Khamenei and President Ebrahim Raisi were both born there. Power irradiates out through Iran from this city.

Until a few years ago, Raisi headed one of the foundations in Mashhad that make up the "parallel State" and control the country's GDP. The Foundation of the Oppressed and Disabled alone controls more resources than the Ministry of Finance. The one that Raisi governed, meanwhile, the Astan Quds Razavi, has assets worth twenty billion dollars, owns pharmaceutical companies, carpet factories, newspapers, insurance companies, and even the license for producing Coca-Cola (Koshgovar).

The young men and women who took to the streets in September 2023 to fight with words, launch Molotov cocktails, let down their hair, and kiss in public are not employees of the State, nor do they work for the so-called private companies held by the foundations. Their parents and grandparents do. For the older generations, protesting meant risking their jobs in a time of economic crisis, with little hope of finding other work.

The situation is different for the seventy percent of Iranians who are thirty-five years old or younger. The economic machine of Iran is jammed; the system that paid salaries to the citizens of the Islamic Republic for decades no longer has room for its youth. The younger generation has had to fend for itself. As a direct consequence, we see the birth, in 2016, of Tapsi, the most widely used ride-sharing platform in Iran; AloPeyk, an online delivery service; Bdood, a bike-sharing app; and Aparat, a local version of YouTube. There's also Digikala, where you can buy and sell clothes online, and Zarinpal, for fast digital payments. There are online networks for people offering lessons in English, math, computer technology, or guitar; networks for people looking for work as cleaners, personal shoppers, cooks, cat sitters, and plant sitters. Young people have created jewelry brands, clothing lines, contemporary Persian carpets, and metalwork, which they sell on local apps or Instagram. Working in a self-managed economy has made them less reliant on the ayatollahs; their salary comes from elsewhere.

Without considering high school students, the mass of protesters was basically made up of people working in the independent economy. The social media profiles of the founders of many startups, such as that of Hessam Armandehi, who invented Iran's version of Uber known as Divar, were filled with messages demanding the liberation of their employees. Their posts included photos of the people who had been arrested while protesting—and they're all around twenty years old. The link was so evident from the outset that the head of the

Telecommunications department of the Revolutionary Guards called for "a clampdown on private startups" immediately after the first protests.

The new Iranians managed to build a parallel and self-sufficient economy out of nothing, one that is sustained by both its employees and its clients; this infuriates the regime both because it exists beyond their control and because it gave rise to the first generation of citizens that does not rely on the ayatollahs for survival, creating the ideal conditions for revolution.

The Illusion

I was riding on the velvet-upholstered night train, heading south towards the desert and the city of Kerman, with my friend Nabila. To save money, we booked two couchettes in a mixed cabin; the other two couchettes were occupied by men. I couldn't sleep because of a stiff neck, she heard me tossing and turning, and offered to give me a neck rub. We had already taken off our veils and were ready for sleep. She climbed on my back to massage my shoulders and neck. If the train conductor had come in, he would have seen her slender body, long fuchsia-hued hair, double-pierced ears, and, peeking out from her tank top, the giant tattoo she has on her back. We were on public transportation, and there were two men in the cabin with us. I was terrified at what might happen if someone slid open the door and found us with our hair down, but she was not the least bit scared.

Nabila is a professional kick-boxer and wrestler, she wins medals across the country. An educated woman, always ready for a fight, she voted conservative. She would have preferred Qasem Soleimani, if he had been alive and had decided to run, to the insipid president Ebrahim Raisi. Nabila is a young woman who is faithful to the Republic of Islam; she is also gay. She follows dozens of Western athlete-influencers on Instagram. Back then, she was especially smitten by Rosamaria Montibeller, a beautiful volleyball player from Brazil with 1.2 million followers who, in addition to playing for the professional Italian team Uyba Volley Busto Arsizio and on the Brazilian national team, is a successful online businesswoman, promoting herself and her three companies—jewelry, clothes, and cosmetics—by modeling and serving as brand ambassador.

Walking down the streets of Tehran, Nabila looked scornfully at women her age in their tight and revealing clothes, all of whom were far more covered up than Rosamaria Montibeller in the photos that Nabila liked on Instagram. "It's not that women's bodies shock me, but I find these girls sad: they're just following trends and don't believe in anything, they don't know who they are or where they come from. The worst ones aren't the rich girls who have been Westernized; they've always been around. The worst are the girls who grew up, like me, in the large apartment blocks in the southern outskirts of the city, girls who stopped dressing carefully and going to mosque, but not for political reasons, just because they wanted other people to think that they were rich, because they wanted to look like those other girls. I like Westerners, but I'm different from them, and proud of it. You won't see me chasing after some exotic lifestyle. Chasing after something is humiliating."

We talked on the day Mahsa Amini died, before the protests began, when the internet still worked. She was furious. She knew perfectly well that what had happened to Mahsa could have happened to her that night on the train to Kerman, or on any other number of nights. Many devout women were traumatized on September 16. While a portion of the population of Iran is radical and militant, an even wider segment supports the Republic of Islam but is not entirely sure that it is right or fair to violently impose headscarves on women who would rather not wear them. For these people, the fact that a girl was stopped in the subway station and returned to her family a corpse a few days later is an obscenity, "a collective humiliation and an immense offense to God," Nabila says.

On September 13, 2022, the religious police stopped Mahsa Amini while she was on vacation in the capital with her parents and her brother. From that moment on, she was under police custody. They ushered her into a van and took her to a police station. They interrogated her and left her in the waiting room. According to the closed-circuit cameras, it was there that she collapsed. When they took her to a hospital, she was in a coma. Two Iranian women journalists rushed to the clinic, talked to her relatives, and took photos. Mahsa never regained consciousness. She died three days later.

The morality police said they never touched her. They said that Mahsa suffered a heart attack. The family says that this is impossible: she was only twenty-two, she was healthy, and she didn't have a heart condition. They also say that the police refused to share the results of the autopsy with them and even asked them not to talk to the press. Actually, they were told they should not talk to anyone. The police asked the family to bury Mahsa at night, in secret, because they were aware of the reaction a public funeral could trigger.

President Raisi promised to carry out a "rigorous investigation," which was supposed to lead to an exemplary punishment for those responsible for her death. The country's leaders publicly paid their respects to the family, and starting that day, the morality police vanished from the streets. Raisi tried to stop the protests before they even started because he knew they would quickly get out of hand. He was less worried about dissidents being the majority, or that they were somehow representative of the country, than he was aware that even the people who didn't want to topple the regime would have been sympathetic to the dissidents' rage, and that, at least initially, they wouldn't have stopped them from expressing themselves.

It was the collective sense of frustration, which transformed into silent and widespread solidarity, that made this protest so persistent and unpredictable, and so very different from any that had come before.

Forouzan told me how they quickly got organized. "We wrote on the walls of all the public bathrooms in Tehran—restaurants, post offices, subway stations, the university—we colonized them all. If you wanted to join the protests for Mahsa, you didn't need the Internet to know when and where to go. All you had to do was walk into any of the public bathrooms in the city."

In addition to flyers and stickers with detailed information about various protests, there were the names of Telegram groups to join, instructions on how to avoid getting arrested, how to protect your phone chats, and how to treat certain kinds of wounds. Protesters could count on the solidarity of strangers. When the police charged them, people who fled could ring the buzzers of random apartments, and someone would inevitably open up for them so they could find refuge. The men chanted: "I'll kill anyone who murders my sister." The women chanted: "Woman, Life, Freedom." The students of Sharif University chose the most offensive chant of all: "Khamenei is worse than Yazid!" Their slogan was particularly harsh because it was tied to tradition; it had nothing to do with foreign propaganda and couldn't be blamed on brainwashing, which is how the authorities explained the rebellion to exonerate themselves. It was also the worst insult they could possibly hurl at the ayatollahs.

Yazid was the killer of Imam Hussein, the son of Ali, the religious leader and martyr who founded the Shiite branch of Islam with his own blood, separating it from the Sunnis when Mohammed's dynasty was split. The martyrdom of Hussein is to Shiites what the Passion of Christ is to Catholics. By choosing that slogan, the students at Sharif University had clearer objectives than any of the other splinter protest groups. They tried to speak to the majority of Iranians who believe in God but who also see and suffer the failings of the Republic of Islam. Their message was: we share a history and we speak the same code; we are protesters, not Martians; but the system does not work, it only weakens us, and it is cruel and dangerous.

The students at Sharif knew that, in terms of an international public, the slogan about Yazid was ineffective because incomprehensible, but their ideas on the matter were clear. They did not nurture any false hopes that foreigners would help them on a practical level, so, at least during this phase, they chose not to focus on the Western press. The most effective thing to do was get the silent majority on board—people who were both disillusioned by the regime and suspicious of alternative makeshift policies and destabilizing forces.

That community of ordinary citizens has already proved capable of changing the destiny of the country several times over, and most recently with the 1979 revolution that was upheld by the majority of Iranians and that initially had, as often happens in such circumstances, a wide range of confused motives. That revolution did not start with the revolt of the clerics but, once the monarchy fell, the clerics won out because, unlike other groups, their members did not disagree on an internal hierarchy, they enjoyed a wide consensus, and they had a widespread presence across the land, able to reach the smallest rural communities of faithful. They were also better organized and more resolute than the Marxists, nationalists, feminists, Maoists, or Islamic socialists.

The Persians had forced another regime to fold when protests broke out in 1891. There was also a revolution in 1911, thanks to which the people won the right to have a Constitution and an elected Parliament. The people even mounted a sweeping uprising in 1951, which failed only because the Shah managed to obtain support from the United States and Great Britain for a coup d'état against Prime Minister Mohammed Mossadeq, who was considered too independent and popular.

"Iranians are not a meek people. They're masters of revolution. It's a question of hitting the right keys," Assim says, aware that revolutions happen by drawing on a range of angers that extend outwards in different directions. "The moment when power crumbles is messy, and the demands of the people get confused. To reach some level of success, everyone's demands need to be maximized. Only afterwards do people decide what shape things will take, only later do they choose the rules of the future."

Iranians initially supported many of the protesters' claims due to widespread dissatisfaction with the status quo. In 2019, there was an uprising in Tehran organized by the indigent, the so-called "shoeless." In 2021, farmers in Isfahan camped out in a stadium to lament the lack of water; the police set their tents on fire, which led to fighting on city streets. "The economic crisis and inflation are felt at all levels, and, for the first time, even by wealthy families like my own. My mother never had to count her pennies when she went out food shopping the way she does now."[3] Non-Persian minority groups, from Kurdistan to Baluchistan, all the way to Khuzestan, stand like "dry haystacks, ready to burst into flames with just a spark."

After Raisi won the election in 2021, many voters lost hope in elections as a way of impacting national politics. "People are angry. A revolution is not like an electoral campaign: we don't start out divided on how to solve the problems. That comes later. Our immediate goal is freedom; later, we'll organize." To Assim, the most significant groups of dissatisfied people are the ones with weapons.

The success of the 1979 revolution can be traced to a specific moment: the Iranian army had already rebelled when, on February 12 of that year, the Shah asked the Air Force to arrest the soldiers who refused to do their duty. The Air Force replied by saying, "We need to remain neutral and let the events take their course." When the pilots betrayed him, the monarchy was finished.

Assim believes a theory that has been circulating in Tehran for some time, but which can only be said in a whisper: no one has the clout or authority necessary to step into the role of Supreme Leader after the now-elderly Ali Khamenei dies, and the Guardians of the Revolution are waiting for that moment to steal the power away from the clerics.

"Do you really think that if you and the Guards ended up on the same side, you'd have the strength to beat them once it is all over?" I ask.

"Whether or not I have faith in our strength is irrelevant. We all know that as long as those with the weapons don't rebel against those with the scepter, the system will never crumble; it might grow weak or dark, but it will remain in its place."

While they're out protesting, Assim's female classmates at Sharif University remove their hijabs, twirl them around their heads, then throw them on a pile with others and light the fabric on fire. They film everything and post it online. On October 2, the police storm the polytechnic, lock the gates with the students and their professors inside, and launch teargas. The protesters scurry underground, towards the parking lots. The police chase after them, shooting rubber bullets that bounce off the walls and strike the moving bodies.

Around this time, a certain kind of game started trending online—the hunt for double standards. It was started by a former Sharif student. The game consists of finding and sharing photos of female family members of the country's leaders without their veils, either abroad or at private parties in Iran, dressed in short skirts or high heels, or outfits with plunging necklines. A number of Khamenei's daughter-in-law's relatives are among the first victims, in particular one of her cousins, who is also the niece of a conservative political philosopher whose ideas have shaped Iranian politics in the recent past.

Meanwhile, in high schools and middle schools, girls from the age of eleven upwards take off their veils and start talking back to the male teachers who dare to scold them. At one middle school, girls throw water and empty plastic bottles at a man, forcing him to cower, retreat, and eventually run away. Suddenly, the police are forced to deal with a new enemy: schoolgirls, minors. A number of officers desert the repression. The young protesters manage to force the police to flee dozens of times. On other occasions, the officers join the protests. The Revolutionary Guards, who number more than a hundred thousand and who theoretically have the power to end the protests with violence in a matter of hours, do not even leave their barracks.

The protests spread in new and different ways compared to those of the past. They unfold in both liberal neighborhoods and conservative towns, large and small, and throughout the provinces populated by religious and ethnic minorities. Everything happens all at once. Assim smells revolution in the air.

He thought it the tide had turned when metalworkers, refinery workers, construction workers, and the electricians who maintain the electrical grid started striking in support of the protests. Even market stalls in the bazaar shut down, and at some point the farmers joined the strike. These two categories of workers—together with the young people who are part of the startup economy—form, in substance, the entire private sector of Iran, considering that the larger companies belong to the foundations that are run by the clerics or Guardians of the Revolution. But it was all an illusion. The workers went on strike because the government hadn't paid their salaries in months, and when the payments started flowing again, they stopped striking. The bazaar merchants rolled down their security gates because they were scared that their shops would be damaged, and not out of support for the protesters.

Keep the Fire Alive

While the students have clear political objectives, the protest is mostly chaotic, poorly coordinated, and all over the place. A video filmed in Karaj, thirty kilometers northeast of Tehran, shows a blood-spattered white pick-up truck belonging to the Basij shortly after being attacked, its front windshield shattered, about to cave in. The camera shifts position, the door to the back seat is open, and a man lies on his side; he is dead. To the right, we see a young man with his face covered, holding a rifle in the air. This scene was filmed during a protest in memory of Hadis Najafi, a TikTokker, born in 2000, who filmed a selfie on September 21, 2022, while walking down the street on her way to join a demonstration. She looks into the camera and says, "I can't wait to watch this in a few years. I'll be happy that I took part in these protests; by then, everything in this country will be different."

Hadis Najafi died in the main square a few hours later. The police shot her six times with real bullets in the chest, face, and neck. Forty days after her death—when the traditional Shiite period of mourning came to an end, at which time people usually travel to the tomb of the deceased to pray—her friends organized a gathering. But they went there seeking revenge, not to pray: they killed the basiji, whose body lies in the truck, while shouting Hadis's name.

In four months, more than sixty Basij agents were killed, and many clerics were attacked. One was knifed and another, in Baluchistan, was executed with a shotgun. In the eastern, and more violent, part of the country, mullahs even started removing their turbans before getting behind the wheel to avoid being targeted by the angry masses.

Starting in late September 2022, in the cities of Tehran, Yazd, Isfahan, and Mashhad, people would open their windows in the middle of the night and start singing protest songs against the Supreme Leader from behind the curtains. Other voices would quickly join in from down the street or block. The Basij sprayed X marks on the buildings where the voices came from, near the intercoms, so that they would remember that as-yet unidentified dissidents lived there.

Forouzan has never been arrested. "But you, on the other hand," she said, turning to look at Assim and away from the camera for a moment, in the park in Chitgar, "did something really stupid."

During one protest march, Assim made the mistake of getting separated from the rest of the group of protesters. A teenage basiji with his face covered shouted at him. Assim started to run, and the young officer shot at him. When Assim stopped, the young basiji caught up, yanked on Assim's hoodie, and made him fall to the ground. Two other basiji soon arrived. Together, they managed to throw Assim into a dark blue minivan. "Young Basij wear masks because we're afraid of them, but they're afraid of us too," Assim says.

A trend that has taken off among the protesters is doxing: if a person manages to take a picture of a basiji, they post it on social media and in Telegram groups; if anyone has details about the identity of that person, they add them to the comments section, with the most sought-after information being where that person lives. This is yet another reason why the people behind the repression cover their faces, at least until they get the protesters into their blue vans and manage to take away their phones.

"At the station house, they stubbed out their cigarettes in our faces. Each time a new basiji came in the room, it started all over again. It was as if each one of them wanted his chance to beat us up, sign their name in bruises on us. They were all younger than me, too. The police stations are the worst; that's where most of the torture happens. People usually confess just so they can be transferred to prison. After the station, the prisons seem like luxury. And when the jailers saw us, they were furious at how badly we'd been beaten up. Basically, you have to try and spend as little time as possible at the police station."

The dirty work is done by the Basij, who are "all very young, often still minors." They earn about a quarter of what the Revolutionary Guards earn, less than three hundred dollars a month, compared to the thousand that the Guards earn. But during the protests of Jin, Jyan, Azadi, not many Guards—in their light-colored khaki camouflage uniforms designed for fighting in desert trenches—were out and about. Instead, they sent the Basij, "brainwashed" teenagers or recruits from extreme Islamic collectives based in high schools and universities. They had never fought anywhere before but were enlisted after the Green Movement of 2009, when the mission was literally to "culturally vaccinate" their peers.[4] In 2009, a problem arose when many of the Revolutionary Guards voted reformist, believing that their votes in the most recent election had been stolen; the fact that members of families with revolutionary credentials joined the street protests against election fraud undermined the rhetoric of the authorities, which cast the Green Movement as "counter-revolutionary."

The first generation of Revolutionary Guards was formed through the Difa'-i muqaddas, the "holy defense"—the armed resistance, to Saddam Hussein's invasion of Iran in 1980. This war began only one year after the Iranian revolution and contributed to the creation of the institutions and the collective conscience of the Republic of Islam. Saddam Hussein thought he could take advantage of the weakness of a still-amorphous State, but the officers fought back; that generation of Revolutionary Guards went off to fight a foreign enemy and often came home with mutilated limbs or the indelible signs of Iraqi chemical weapons. They tolerated fatigue, fear of death, and major wounds in the belief that they were protecting all Iranians with their bodies. Back then, they did not use violence against their own people. With the protests of 2009, a new class of agents of repression was created, people who didn't have the experience or history of revolution, but who were deeply committed to ideology. From that point on, the "young Basij" felt entitled to explain the revolution in polemical and militant tones to the older generations of Revolutionary Guards who had actually fought in the revolution.[5]

I met with a first-generation Revolutionary Guard in Tehran, a man who came back without legs from the trenches in the 1980s. "The younger the soldiers, the more dangerous and disconnected from reality they are," he explained. "We know very well what violence is from what we were forced to endure, we were vaccinated against its presumed allure. We know how to calibrate it, how to avoid it when possible. These kids have never been afraid of dying, they have never fully experienced violence, they don't even realize what they're doing when they inflict it on others: they're fanatics, they lack all judgment."

Forouzan and Assim tell me about the moment when the most spontaneous phase of the protests came to an end. "The first executions started in December. They were traumatic, a breaking point. We never thought things would come to that," Forouzan says.

He interrupts her. "You can't say their method wasn't effective; after the first hanging, a lot of people were scared off."

Forouzan and Assim used to meet up with other protesters in the same parts of Tehran as Mohsen Shekari, the first dissident who was executed. Shekari was twenty-three years old, he shared an apartment with a friend, worked in a café, and wrote rap music and lyrics. When he was hanged, protest groups on Telegram were filled with messages, such as: "It's not true. Don't let them trick us. They're trying to scare us, to force us to give up. No one knows who this kid is. Don't believe their propaganda." Other messages followed suit: "If anyone knows who this kid is, speak up." Forouzan was one of several who spoke up. Initially, the protesters couldn't and didn't want to believe that he had really been hanged. At first, they thought it was theatrics, psychological terrorism. But it was true.

"Shekari's case was assigned to a monster known as 'the psychopath.' We know all the judges, we know everything about them," Assim says. Your life depends on what part of the city you're arrested in, so it's dangerous to even go outside a certain jurisdiction. "I was lucky, I have a suspended sentence. But if I get arrested again, they'll lock me up for six years."

Another twenty-three-year-old, Majidreza Rahnavard, was executed on December 12, 2022, in Mashhad. He was not killed in prison behind closed doors, which is what usually happens in the Republic of Islam when someone is condemned to death, such as drug dealers or people guilty of murder or bloodshed. Rahnavard was hanged from a construction crane, and a video of the execution was disseminated by the Mizan news agency. In it, the executioners wear black masks and ski goggles; Rahnavard is dressed in a white tunic, and his hands are tied behind his back. Rahnavard was poor, he worked at a fruit and vegetable shop, he was an amateur athlete, a wrestler. His mother went to visit him in prison a few days before the execution and said that he was in good form, that he smiled, which led her to believe that her son thought that he'd soon be released. He didn't say as much because he wasn't sure, she said, he didn't want to jinx it, that was the only possible explanation for his smile. She had gone home reassured, calmer. The real reason for his smile, though, was that Rahnavard knew he was going to die, and he didn't want his mother to remember their last encounter as a sad one. She learned that he had been condemned only after the hanging; someone recorded her wailing with their smartphone. Forouzan connected the audio clip to a speaker placed on a balcony in Tehran, and her tragic cries were played on a loop for the whole night.

Forouzan and Assim never thought that things would come

to this. The violence that took place out on the streets or in prisons was one thing, but public executions were something else entirely. The former was used as a form of propaganda, the latter was a show of pure cruelty. The fact that the hangings were no longer hidden behind prison walls but done in public with the goal of intimidation, and that videos were circulated showing the executioner and the bound victims only a few moments before their death, was "a newly rediscovered form of horror designed to terrify us."

After the first execution of a protester who'd been accused of killing a basiji, the Iranian student groups started asking themselves some difficult questions. What could the rest of the world do for them now? "We talked about it often, but there was no consensus. A lot of us here are angry at how people abroad claim they support the protests, but they're not risking anything. The Iranian diaspora abroad, the organizations that back the monarchy, and the pseudo communists were all stuck in another political era.[6] Some of them spoke up on our behalf without our consent, without even consulting us, saying that, first and foremost, we wanted harsher sanctions on Iran. There is not a single Iranian protester here who would say that tougher sanctions are the first point on our list. We've been living under sanctions for years, and the families who govern this country continue to live in their luxurious villas, while other families have lost a great deal. I wish there were a way of isolating the people in power without isolating the country, but we're realistic. We know that ending up isolated, like North Korea, is a trap and not a guarantee of freedom."

Eyes Everywhere and the Berlin Wall

The threat of an uncontrollable reaction by a generation who wanted nothing to do with the laws of the Republic of Islam led the authorities to develop new systems of policing and control. Starting in 2020, Iran worked on a pilot project with China. In

August 2022, a few weeks before Mahsa Amini was stopped in a subway station for wearing her veil slightly askew, an Iranian official admitted, for the first time, that cameras had been set up that were programmed with algorithms to find women who were not wearing their hijabs correctly. They positioned these cameras at night on ATM machines, on slides in playgrounds, in public offices, at intersections, and in subway stations. The technology was provided by Tiandy, a leader in AI-powered video-surveillance, based in Tientsin, south of Beijing.

This company is altering the public spaces of Iran, placing eyes in every corner, as the head of the police Admad-Reza Radan, has said. The goal of the project is to make the repression more ambiguous, quieter. To get inside people's homes before revolt can break out in the streets. To use less tear gas and more intelligence. To find out early on who the rebels are, and go knock on their doors. This will let the authorities quash outdoor protests and prevent them from inspiring others, putting out the spark before it can lead to a fire. It also means less use of truncheons on the street, acts of violence that anger the more devout families who are generally not, or only a little, opposed to the regime.

On July 5, 2022, President Ebrahim Raisi announced new rules and tighter controls on "veils and chastity," which were then passed to the Ministry for the Propagation of Virtue and the Repression of Vice in Tehran. One month later, the authorities announced the presence of smart cameras and began to threaten girls, explaining that punishments would be straightforward and automatic: they would no longer be able to withdraw cash from ATM machines or go to public offices to pay their university fees; their passports and licenses would be revoked; if they worked for the State, they would lose the possibility of getting a raise or end-of-year bonus. At the end of September, after one week of protests, the head of the Judicial and Legal Commission of Parliament, Mousa Ghazanfari Abadi, said that they needed to speed up the installation of cameras with facial recognition to reduce the clashes between police and protesters. After the first major protest, he wanted to avoid a second one, and possible bloodshed.

At that point in time, they used a technique that was based on identifying the protesters, the organizers, and their leaders. They then investigated their network of connections on social media and arrested them in secret, to prevent ideas from spreading. At that point, they either convinced them to stop what they were doing or forced them to do so.

While speaking to journalists and responding to criticism from the Iranian press about how he handled the protests, Ghazanfari Abadi asked the public for time and trust, going on to make a promise that sounded to the protesters like a threat. "The use of face recording cameras can systematically implement this task and reduce the presence of the police, as a result of which there will be no more clashes between the police and citizens."[7] In April 2023, the police announced they had installed new video cameras. From that moment on, people who were identified through video analysis received their first warning on their cell phones.

Forouzan thought this was a clever move on the part of the ayatollahs. "A new system of surveillance with a capillary structure would mean that any sign of rebellion, however small or isolated, could be swiftly identified and punished. The government would be able to isolate sparks and extinguish them before they flared up in unison again. Naturally, we've already thought of a way to keep the fire burning."

They started taking part in various social media challenges. As of April 2023, three are ongoing in Iran. The first is the most basic: a woman and a man need to be photographed together from the back, the woman without a veil, and the husband or boyfriend with his arm around her waist. The second challenge requires the help of a friend to do the filming: a woman wearing a hijab has to walk through the subway turnstile in front of the Guards, remove her veil as soon as she passes through the gates, and get onto the train with her long hair flowing. The third challenge is the riskiest: a woman has to either take a selfie or have a friend photograph her standing next to the police without her hijab.

While the massive protests in streets may have stopped, young Iranian women—from the capital of Tehran to the conservative and holy city of Masshad all the way to the provinces of Kurdistan—are using their smartphones to film and share individual actions that, gathered together under the same hashtag, are equivalent to a long procession of thousands of women without their veils. These new forms of protest mirror the changing methods of policing and repression.

On April 15, Radan, the Chief of the national police, who had been named four months earlier to deal with the Jin, Jiyan, Azadi movement, joined the rest of the authorities in declaring that fewer police and more technology were needed to enforce the rule of the veil. From that moment forward, "non-conforming" women and girls were identified with closed-circuit video cameras and received a notification, but not a punishment. If they continued not to wear their hijab, they were fined. New video cameras were even installed along the highway to check on the women in cars; if they weren't wearing their headscarves, the cars were confiscated.

Around that same time, a historic bookstore was shut down for selling books and magazines to girls without their veils. Similar situations had already taken place in music shops, cafés, hotels, game arcades, and gyms. Radan said that those who instigate women not to cover up were guiltier than the women themselves, indicating the owners of those businesses.[8] Since punishing the women was not working, they shifted the onus onto the people who stood in solidarity with them, who let them do what they wanted. In so doing, they managed to isolate women once again.

Following Radan's comments, an Iranian woman with a long red braid recorded a video of herself in which she spoke directly to the head of the police. In the short film, you see only a part of her face and her long hair. "I heard your threats," the woman says, "but you've been threatening us for forty-four years. You explained the punishments that await us, but you've been punishing us for forty-four years. You have killed us, you have shot us in the face with your rubber bullets to blind us, you have kidnapped us, arrested us, and never let us go, but you do not scare us. Whatever threat you utter today to frighten us, you have already done much worse. It hasn't worked. We wouldn't still be here today if it had. You have no more cards to play; let the games begin."

Under the proposed new rules, the most severe punishment for women who continued to refuse to wear their veils, even after being fined, would be the end of certain social rights, and chief among them the right to education. In a country where the majority of the university students are female, this would be perceived as a major wrong. It would gravely offend all Iranians, including Sakine Sadat Paad, a conservative and political adviser to President Ebrahim Raisi. In a rare show of support, she spoke up in public to say that inflicting a punishment of this kind on girls who don't wear hijabs is "above all, unconstitutional." She then went on to explain: "The violation of the rules [by women] cannot be punished with equally illegal, non-Islamic, and completely irrational decisions [by us in the government]." She was the first woman in government to explicitly criticize a government proposal against women.[9]

Since Mahsa Amini's death, the Iranian authorities have often been split on how to respond to this unprecedented protest movement. Many ayatollahs consider the hijab a kind of Berlin wall, whereby: a hijab is important not just for what it is, but for its symbolism; if we surrender something that is—or appears to be, for those on the outside—essential to us, that small rift could eventually bring us all down, like the first strike of a pick-axe against the Berlin Wall, which caused the entire Soviet Union to crumble. But only a part of the regime sees it this way.

There is low consensus for the severe punishment of young women in Iran, even among those who theoretically ought to mete it out, namely the conservatives and clerical leaders.

II.
The Ayatollahs

> "If you want to arrest a woman because she is not wearing her veil, arrest me instead."
> —Ayatollah Hossein Ansarian, on the Iranian State-controlled television during Ramadan, April 2023.[10]

One of the first pushbacks you're likely to face as a Western journalist in Iran is against a widespread simplification: the idea that power in Iran functions perfectly. That orders sent downstream reach the person in charge of executing them unmodified. That rules are unequivocally enforced. That the clerics and the police see eye to eye, that they have a collaborative relationship. That all clerical leaders stand united. That a broader notion of politics does not exist—that while power struggles within the government are acknowledged, it is not generally accepted that people in leadership have divergent and conflicting visions for the country, expressed with sincere ambition. That the regime functions as a systematically lethal unit. That Parliament acts unanimously, with a single voice. That the Ministry of Foreign Affairs pursues, with different tools, the same goals as the Quds forces of the Revolutionary Guards. That censorship works.

The older generations of Basij soldiers hate the younger

ones, and the feeling is mutual. The descendants of the founder, Ruhollah Khomeini, have an ongoing dispute with the Revolutionary Guards of today after they dared to humiliate the children of the paramilitary group's founder in public. There are constant harsh internal struggles among the people in charge of the State-run media agencies on how exactly the Revolution should be communicated in this day and age. A number of other newspapers publish articles that the authorities do not want to read. When Iranians welcome people from the West into their country, they are amused by our way of seeing the regime, how we simplify it to such a degree that it is disfigured.

We have already discussed how only some of the people in power in Iran consider the hijab a question of life or death, their own personal Berlin Wall; we have pointed out how scant agreement exists on the issue of serving up harsh punishments for young women, even by those who should enforce them. Indeed, following Mahsa Amini's death, clerical leaders of the conservative wing asked for the abolition of the morality police, and the Great Ayatollah of the holy city of Qom, Asadolla Bayat-Zanjani, denounced the agents' behavior as "against the law, against God, against all logic."[11]

But the most incredible comments came from the morality police themselves. The spokesperson for the headquarters of the Gasht-e Ershad said, basically, that criminalizing those who wear their veils poorly or barely is pointless, that arresting women only furthers tension and creates enemies within the Iranian population. They declared that removing one's veil should not be considered a crime, but, if anything, an administrative violation. Overseeing cultural issues such as these is the responsibility of schools, they say, and not the police force. Basically, they said: Dear leaders, if you can't convince women to wear headscarves, we, the police, cannot help you. It's a fascinating case of an institution that repudiates itself.

This is significant because the Republic of Islam is not a theocracy; the law imposed is not that of God, but of men.[12] There's a Constitution, a civil code, a penal code, and a commercial code, all of which were, in part, inspired by European legal code books. The first draft of the Constitution was drafted by Ayatollah Khomeini on the basis of the French Constitution. And it was very liberal, far more than the one that came later, and all because of a mistake made by Iranian "liberals," who insisted with Khomeini that the charter be written by an assembly of officials elected by the people, not merely submitted to a plebiscite once it had been written up. Considering that the clergy had an extensive organization and enjoyed strong popular support, they earned a crushing majority from the Assembly and produced a Constitution that was far less liberal than the one initially offered to the liberals by conservative Khomeini.

The constitution that was finally put up for a referendum and approved by a wide majority in 1979 contained the principle of *Velayat-e faquih*, an element which was not present in Khomeini's draft.[13] This principle, which means "protected by iuris peritus"—in other words, the ayatollahs—allowed power to be handed over to the clerics, placing limits on popular sovereignty in Iran. This, in turn, led to a split within the institutions. On the one side, there were the members of parliament and the president, all elected figures, while on the other side were the wise clerics, who were given control of all aspects of life in the Shiite community.

The position of the Supreme Leader is unique in how the system lets him have the final word on everything, to reap praise when things go well, and to blame elected figures when they do not. Iranians were angered by the incompetence of Ahmadinejad's populist government when the country fell into an economic crisis, even if the Supreme Leader could have enacted policies that would have changed the outcome, but did not. Iranians used their votes to punish the reformist president

Rouhani for getting tricked by the Americans when the nuclear deal fell apart and tough new sanctions were put into place—even if that deal would never have existed without the blessing of the Leader. The Supreme Leader never loses. And the Supreme Leader is the only head of State in the world to be formally granted a certain kind of superpower: the right to lie.

This immense power, combined with a substantial lack of responsibility, may be the exact opposite of our Western conception of democracy, but one of its implications is that it allowed Ali Khamenei to make a surprising about-face on the question of the veil. The head of the Republic of Islam can always change his mind without fearing consequences. During the protests, he denied that he had ever established a well-known doctrine nicknamed "Fire at will," which was based on never capitulating and always responding to rebellions and proposed cultural changes with maximum harshness. He actually tweeted, "The issue is not the hijab," going on to say that the girls who choose not to wear headscarves are not necessarily bad citizens of the Republic of Islam.[14]

The Persians are an Indo-European people, not Arab. Shiites are a minority of Islam; the only beliefs they share with other Muslims around the world are that Allah is the only god, that Muhammad is his prophet, and that the Koran is a sacred text. While Sunnis also base their religious practice on the actions of the Prophet and the teachings that form the Sunna, for the Shiites, the ayatollahs are the reflection of God on earth, and men of their time. As a result, any limits that exist on popular sovereignty are not rules carved in stone or written in a book, but rather whatever religious leaders deem to be right and indispensable in the era they live in. The Islamic Republic, therefore, has the capacity of modifying the rules according to politics, which is to say, depending on what Iranian men and women think and want, as it has in the past.

The Koran says nothing about women having to cover their heads; while all four Sunni schools of law consider the hijab an obligation, the Islamic Republic does not recognize or follow those interpretations.[15] After the Revolution, but before headscarves were obligatory, Iranian clerics were divided on the matter: some considered the rule unnecessary, a mistake that would eventually backfire on the people who imposed it. Since the early days of the regime, prominent jurists, like Mohammad Beheshti, or theologians, such as Mahmoud Taleghani, were against making the veil compulsory. The law was not central to the plan or vision of those who backed Khomeini. Actually, the first real law on compulsory headscarves only appeared in 1983, four years after the Revolution.[16]

While the Sunnis accuse the Shiites of heresy, the Shiites are proud of their non-dogmatic approach and, in turn, accuse the Sunnis of having spawned extremist, inflexible Salafi and Wahabi groups such as Al Qaeda and the Islamic State. This explains the existence of ayatollahs, both during the Revolution and today, who are openly opposed to the rule of headscarves for women, and yet no one in Iran would dare label them "infidels." This is why the abolition of the law of compulsory headscarves is not, theoretically speaking, impossible—even without a regime change.

Everyone knows about the party scene in Tehran and the raves that take place in the desert. The clerics and government institutions alike have tolerated them for decades. The fact that people plant grapes in their private, walled gardens is also well-known—after all, they're visible to policemen from the outside—but warrants are rarely issued to enter into people's homes to uproot the vines, unless it is to frame a political dissident. The goal is to punish dissent, not the private pursuit of pleasure.

Respect for how private individuals choose to find pleasure is not tantamount to shutting an eye. As the conservative Nabila, with her fuchsia hair and tattoo, points out: "It's a pillar of Shia culture! It's a way of keeping public and private separate, it's about concealment, hiding and disguising oneself, pretending and lying." That which is a sin in the West is a value in Shia culture.

Hooman Majd, an Iranian writer who lives in New York and whose articles stand out for their irony, once wrote: "American presidents Nixon, Clinton, and Bush regret not being born Shia for one reason: the freedom to tell lies without paying the consequences."[17] This is the Supreme Leader's superpower: he can lie to everyone. This principle is deeply rooted in the history of the Iranian people, who had to hide to protect themselves from persecution by the Sunni majority, and who have since managed to elevate ambiguity to a noble value. Nabila frequently reminds me that lying to others can be a holy act but that it's a sin to lie to oneself: "Even the Koran says that we must lie for the benefit of others." In fact, *Taqiyya* is a pillar of the Shiite religion; it means hiding one's faith from strangers in anticipation of the dangers that sincerity might bring. Denying one's beliefs is not just permissible; in some circumstances, it is a religious duty.[18]

Shiites refer to the current period of waiting for the Savior as "occultation." They consider hiding, mystification, and duplicity as traditions and virtues. If you want to understand how irreconcilable elements coexist in Iran, you need to be aware of these principles. They're the same ones that allow Nabila to guiltlessly weave together her private life as a libertine and her public identity as a young woman faithful to the Islamic Revolution. "My behavior is not rebellious: people who see contradictions in my world are those who want to simplify it. They just don't understand."

White Dishes

Before we had the Internet on our smartphones, if you looked at Iran from the skies above, you saw broad expanses of white satellite dishes. Clusters of them indicated villages, thousands of them meant a large city. The authorities of the Islamic

Republic have been blaming each other for more than a decade for not having done more to stem the epidemic of white dishes despite being aware of how dangerous and contagious they were.[19] The dishes held the West in capsule form. They were lightweight, easy-to-transport, relatively inexpensive, and could be installed in an afternoon on a terrace or balcony railing.

In a matter of years, private satellite antennas cracked open the revolutionary rhetoric and allowed Rupert Murdoch—the Australian-American tycoon and owner of Sky, 21st Century Fox, Fox News, as well as Farsi1, a network designed for a Persian audience but based in Dubai—to sneak in.[20] Murdoch brought a wide range of shows to Iran: everything from "How I Met Your Mother" to Turkish soap operas to Italian crime dramas. Before the revolutionary channel Farsi1 appeared, there were television series in Iran, but they followed a rigorous code. If there was a character without a beard, you could be sure he was a villain; sometimes he even had a pre-Islamic Persian name like Cyrus or Darius, a throwback to when there was an Empire but no Koran. The good guy, with whom you inevitably empathized thanks to the scriptwriters, always had a beard and was therefore a good Muslim.

If you head down Vali Asr Boulevard, which divides Tehran in two from north to south, at the very top, you'll find the richer, more secular neighborhoods, people driving Audis and women in tight jeans, the mosques half-empty even on Fridays. At the lower end of the street, you'll see women in dark veils and members of the working class. A man with four daughters who lives at the southern end of the street said to me: "The first clean-shaven Cyrus who was also the hero—I saw him in a Latin American soap opera on Farsi1." Without realizing it, Rupert Murdoch had brought him into the homes of the Islamic Republic.

In 550 BC, Cyrus founded the first Persian Empire, which stretched from Libya to Crimea in the west, and all the way to the Chinese border in the east. At half a million square kilometers, it was larger than the Roman Empire in its glory days. Cyrus ruled over half the population of the planet, something that had never happened before and would never happen again in the history of the world. His dynasty lasted for nearly two centuries, until Darius III was tricked by Alexander the Great.

The Islamic Republic has mixed feelings towards that grand monarchical legacy. On the one hand, a glorious past helps keep nationalism alive. On the other, the ayatollahs are, after all, revolutionaries who managed to drive out the king with clubs, sticks, and the rage of the people not more than forty years ago.

Darius III and his wife later converted to Zoroastrianism, the religion founded by the prophet Zarathustra, which, at the leader's encouragement, spread through the empire until it became a majority religion. In September 2022, when the widespread protests began, embracing the Kurdish feminist slogan "Woman, Life, Freedom," large groups of young Iranians chose to further antagonize their leaders by converting in the streets from Islam to Zoroastrianism. For a while, they even started going to temples.

During one of my trips to Iran, I visited the Zoroastrian Fire Temple in Yazd. Beyond the oval reflection pool, the white staircase, and the porticoes—where a stylized stone eagle stares down at visitors from its perch—is the main room, with its eternally burning "victory fire." Iran is a semi-theocracy, and as such, it does not forbid people from professing other religions than that of the State. While Saudi Arabia only allows mosques, the Islamic Republic of Iran has more than six hundred active churches and, in the capital alone, eleven synagogues.

While the Jewish community in Iran is the largest in the entire Middle East (excluding Israel, obviously), the Islamic Republic forces Iranian Jews to accept an unwritten rule that says "we will finance Jewish schools and Jewish hospitals with public money and guarantee you seats in Parliament regardless of the outcome of the elections, but you have to repudiate the idea of Israel, and live as if it did not exist."

Situated only a few kilometers apart from each other in Tehran are a Jewish school, which is financed by the ayatollahs, and a small factory, responsible for producing the highest number of Israeli flags in the world after the Jewish state, but with one key purpose—to set them on fire. Occasionally, these flags are also set out in an orderly manner, creating a giant carpet, and then trampled on during rallies, where children's entertainment includes shooting at portraits of Israeli Prime Minister Benjamin Netanyahu with rifles loaded with tomatoes in place of bullets.

The white dishes contrast sharply with Tehran's official rhetoric about the black veils. Black not only represents religion, tradition, and mourning, it also primarily stands for misery. It is the color of the poor, or of respect for the poor, of humility, piety, and protection. The noun *chadori*—which comes from the term *chador*, or the dark, opaque, sack-like, head-to-toe veil with a hole at face-level—is used to refer equally to a religious woman, a working-class woman, and to a peasant woman.

During the 1978 Revolution, protests against the Shah led to martial law. Then, one Friday, the military shot and killed more than a hundred protesters in Jaleh Square. That day went down in history as "Black Friday," both for the mourning that followed but also to describe the dark abyss into which the monarchy fell. For Iranians, the hashtag #BlackFriday has an entirely different meaning than the one we are familiar with. No one in Iran uses it to refer to a shopping day—and people even get outraged when Westerners do.

Black also functions as the symbolic opposite of the "modernization" and "Westernization" that was ushered in by the monarchy in the 1960s with the so-called "White Revolution."

The uprising that deposed the Shah in 1979, and saw power be transferred into the hands of clerics, was sustained by communists, nationalists, the Islamic feminist movement, and by the kind of women who had been wearing the chador for centuries. Initially, these women had been encouraged by the Shah to wear their veils and were only later told to remove them, when they were effectively banned in public. Since then and until the measure was repealed, devout women were faced with a dilemma each time they wanted to leave the house: end up at the police station or in hell. To avoid having to choose, some women stopped going out entirely. If they held jobs, they quit.

In the 1970s, a large portion of the population saw the Shah's policies as a blessing, but after 1979, a majority of those people left the country and became part of the enormous Iranian diaspora. Four million people fled, with one in ten now living in California. After that cultural and political community broke off from the rest of society, and after the great exodus, the ayatollahs had an easier time projecting a credible image of a unified people under their leadership. In 2009, they had a revelation: "The youth of this country no longer understands revolutionary language. We're wasting our time on propaganda." Thanks to research into conversations and documents done by Narges Bajoghli and published by Stanford University Press, we have learned just how concerned the media of the regime was about the youth, thirteen years before the protests for Mahsa Amini began.[21]

The revelation came about during the Green Movement of 2009, the protest against electoral fraud that had handed another presidential term to the populist-conservative leader Mahmoud Ahmadinejad, instead of the reformist candidate Mir-Hossein Mousavi. With protests taking place in the street, the political apparatus had a series of emergency meetings, during which someone made the following comment: "If we don't become more flexible, we lose the entire system. The future is theirs because of their sheer numbers. They outnumber us."

A famous director of propaganda films added: "I talk about

this all the time with my filmmakers. We've lost the youth in our country. We need to face this reality." Among the first-generation Revolutionary Guards, men who had experienced the Islamic Revolution as boys, one noticed that the protesters of 2009 were shouting some of the same slogans as in 1979: "Down with the dictator!" His children were in the crowds out on the street.

"Madam Vice President"

"Divorce existed in Iran even before our Revolution, but it was an abstract concept, never applied. If you got divorced, your husband kept the children; they became his property, and he could choose not to let you see them ever again, even out of spite. As a result, no one got divorced. Today, after our Revolution, children are not separated from their mothers, and this has changed everything: now, women who want to leave their husbands do."

In Tehran, in the summer of 2021, I met with the most powerful woman in the country, Masoumeh Ebtekar, a reformist political leader and a Muslim feminist who was then the vice-president of Iran. After leaving my backpack and laptop with the security forces, and after a very long and thorough search, we met in her office.

Masoumeh Ebtekar is petite and has large eyes. In the official group photographs that hang on her walls, the leaders of the republic stand solemnly around her with grim expressions, but she always smiles. We met in a conference room with a large oval table in the middle; she stood up when I walked in, said "Buongiorno" in shaky Italian, and offered me a cappuccino, which is to say a powdered Nestlé product that gets mixed with hot water in a semblance of a cappuccino.

Generally, Iranians drink tea during meetings. The offering of a cappuccino was her way of saying: look at the care and respect I have for you, an Italian, by including your drink on the tray of our traditional drinks. While I would have preferred tea, I naturally accepted the cappuccino.

Iranians are excessively polite. Their brand of politeness can easily unsettle a Westerner, and they often use it as a kind of test. They almost never get to the point and even if they do, you are forced to first engage in endless small talk, which they consider good manners. The directness and clarity that we appreciate so much are considered vulgar and synonymous with haste.

In reply to her comments on divorce, I told her how my high school English teacher, a feminist who had taken part in the 1968 protests and who was still stuck in that era, used to say, "Cecilia, the person who invented the washing machine did more for us women than the Ministry of Equal Opportunities." What she meant was that without that tool taking the place of handwashing, women would never have had time to read, study, work, or leave the house. Society would have changed much more slowly. She was telling me that certain practical details, all far less exciting than slogans, were capable of bringing about swifter changes than laws passed by Parliament. Masoumeh Ebtekar nodded as if to say, *Good, I see you understand.*

But then I added how hard it was for me to understand how someone like her, an internationally renowned scientist, a well-educated woman, the most powerful woman in Iran, still needed written consent from her husband—who was far less important than she was—to leave the country. For a moment, she didn't say anything. Then she smiled and said, "I don't understand why everyone got so excited when Kamala Harris was named the first woman vice-president of the United States in 2021. I became vice-president here, for the first time, in 1997." She then went on to mention how, in certain Islamic countries, and here she was referring to Saudi Arabia, women have only just recently earned the right to drive cars, while women in Iran have been flying planes for years. I interrupted her before she went on to tell me about all the wonderful women taxi drivers in Tehran; we could have kept playing that game for days. I knew she'd never admit that gender apartheid still exists in the country where she'd been ruling for so long.

Masoumeh Ebtekar speaks English with an American accent. She sounds like a native speaker. Not only does she know it, but she chooses to speak it with a foreigner like me, not an insignificant fact for a representative of a country that often refers to the United States as "Great Satan." It is a question of form and protocol; one does not speak in public or with the press in the language of the enemy. But Masoumeh Ebtekar grew up in Upper Darby, just outside Philadelphia, and her father was a student at the University of Pennsylvania. Everyone in her family is a scientist, and she has a PhD in Immunology. She returned to Iran as soon as she became an adult and went on to enroll at Iranzamin, an Iranian and American international school in Tehran. That's when she started to wear a long, dark chador. She did it for religious reasons and in the name of political activism. When, in 1978, university students started to knock down the statues of the Shah, Ebtekar was among them. And when those who opposed the Shah started rallying around the charismatic figure of Khomeini, who sent audio cassettes from exile in Paris inciting people to revolt, she helped distribute them around the capital. Ebtekar was a front-line participant in the Revolution, literally and figuratively.

Then, on November 4, 1979, came the rupture between the two countries that, until that point, Masoumeh Ebtekar had considered her home. It was an event so huge that it has soured relations between Americans and Iranians for over forty years. Militant students stormed the US embassy in Tehran, took the Marines and the CIA by surprise, and fooled them: the front lines protesting on the other side of the barbed wire fence that surrounded the embassy were comprised of women, with Ebtekar in the lead. Under their chadors they hid hammers, pincers, and clubs to use against the American military in case the soldiers resisted. But the Marines had no intention of firing into a mass of unarmed young protesters, and as a result, they were overthrown. This humiliating event marked the political life of then-Democratic President Jimmy Carter and left a wound in Washington that has never entirely healed.

In their off-limits area within the embassy, the men and women of the CIA started to furiously burn their secret documents. A handful of students, with Masoumeh acting as spokeswoman, took fifty-two Americans hostage, whom they held captive for what seemed like an infinite amount of time: 444 days. These were not defenseless tourists, but civil servants, soldiers, and spies. There were protests in the United States, with one of the most popular signs at rallies calling on the White House for reprisal with an absurd demand: "Deport all Iranians!"

Inside the US embassy in Tehran, Masoumeh was in charge of talking to the Americans: she threatened, consoled, negotiated, and translated from English to Farsi and vice versa throughout the entire hostage period. The American press nicknamed her "Mary." In Ben Affleck's blockbuster hostage crisis film *Argo*, the character "Tehran Mary" is based on Ebtekar.

Her real name, Masoumeh, means "innocent." It does not suit her. In 2019, she was part of the government that responded to the "shoeless" protests over rising fuel prices by sending in the Basij to suppress them, with hundreds dying in the streets. Although the American embassy in Iran has been closed for more than forty years, Masoumeh demanded access to it for her wedding day, and was granted entry; her guests ate to their hearts' content and danced in its courtyard, showing caustic mockery. Still today, graffiti on the wall near the embassy says, "Let the Americans be angry with us, let them die in rage."

Masoumeh Ebtekar was editor in chief of a major newspaper, the "Kayhan International." She founded the Institute for Women's Studies and Research. In 2014, she chaired the 12th International Congress of Immunology in the city of Ahvaz. She was the first woman to hold office in the Islamic government—in the late 1990s, when President Mohammad Khatami's reformists were in power. When I met her, she was at the end of her third mandate as Vice-President.

To this day, and for everyone, she is "Madam Vice President." Always in English, and often with malice. Mostly because of her upbringing, but also because her relationship with the United States has flourished of late, with her son studying for his doctorate in Los Angeles. "Americans have a thousand wonderful qualities, as does their country. Just think of my passion for the sciences, which my father also loved, and my son, too. They are the pioneers in innovation and technology. But choosing to study there and enjoying all the opportunities the United States has to offer does not mean that we agree with Washington's foreign policy." She told me that she is not at all afraid for her son. "Just as I have no fear for the poisonous gossip that may surround me, for my relationship with the United States, here in Iran." The vice-president smiles. She knows better than to justify herself. In Iran, any justification sounds like an admission of guilt. As the famous saying goes: "If you say something, I believe you; if you repeat it, I begin to get suspicious; if you swear it's true, I know you're lying."

"I took part in the Revolution. Before me, my father took to the streets against the coup that deposed Mossadeq. He was a much-loved prime minister, perhaps too much so. He had popular support, but the monarch did not. The prime minister was eliminated by the Shah with vital assistance from the British and Americans," Ebtekar says. It was then that Iranians started to mistrust the United States; their mistrust of the British was already deeply rooted. Even today, when you want to say that someone is plotting something, whether at work or at home, you say, "There's something British going on here." In Iran, it's quite common to encounter conspiracy theorists. A generally accepted explanation for the presence of this syndrome, with its feelings of entrapment and paranoia, dates back to when Shiites were a persecuted minority in Islam and had to live in hiding.

Khalil Tahmassebi was a follower of Supreme Leader Ali Khamenei, when, in 1951, at the age of twenty-six, he murdered then Prime Minister Ali Razmara as he was leaving the mosque after prayers. Razmara was a military general, he had been tasked with further centralizing power in the hands of Shah Mohammad Reza and strengthening ties with the British. Upon his death, Mohammad Mossadeq was elected to power; he had promised to nationalize oil. For many, this was seen as an attempt to liberate their country from its role as a never-ending gas pump for the British. As a matter of fact, for the previous forty years, all of Iran's oil had belonged to the United Kingdom; England fought WWI with a naval fleet that ran entirely on Iranian fuel. In the 1940s, bars and restaurants still existed in Iran that had signs that said "No Dogs or Iranians." Many British, employees of the Anglo-Iranian Oil Company, lived in Iran with their families and did not want to mix with the locals; those bars and restaurants were just for them.

Mossadeq wanted to nationalize oil and take it away from the British. He followed a different line of thinking than the assassinated General Razmara, and believed that the Shah should rule but not govern, as European monarchies do today, as London has essentially taught us. The American and British governments got in the way. In August 1953, in a joint intelligence operation codenamed "Ajax," they deposed Prime Minister Mossadeq. This marked the beginning, in Iran, of anti-American sentiments, anti-capitalist beliefs, and the notion that the Shah was no longer the king of Persia, but someone who answered to foreigners. Nationalists, Marxist left-wing groups, and the clerics rode the tide of this rage.

"'This is our country; what do those foreigners want?' people asked themselves in a genuine, even naive way," Ebtekar tells me. After Mossadeq was deposed, Shah Mohammad Reza felt threatened by his own people and grew even more paranoid and violent. "There was a precise moment when many people's way of looking at America changed. For me, it was the day when, after the coup, Savak—the monarchy's secret police—started torturing Mossadeq supporters like my own father. Our relationship with the United States is not just political, it's personal."

The same country that had welcomed her father, allowed him to study, and allowed him to become a scientist and a wealthy man, was now underwriting his torturers. But even after the Shah fell and Masoumeh and her fellow revolutionaries won their cause, torture did not end.

In the 1980s, dissidents in Iran were first taken to local prisons scattered around the country, and kept in cells where the sounds of other people being tortured were often sufficient to obtain mass confessions. Then, after they'd been divided into small groups, the detainees were put on trucks or trains and taken to Evin prison in Tehran. When monarchists heard the words "you will now be taken to the capital," they knew they would soon be killed and they started to scream, but the communists did not.[22] Communists remembered the Savak, the Shah's secret police, and the political prisoners they had executed or tortured until they "disappeared," but they thought that the Shia clerics with whom they had shared a revolution were not capable of such things. The royalists were right and the communists were wrong.

Often, entire families were considered dissidents, including many young couples, and some even with children. Among them were the parents of my friend Nasim, owner of the house where I danced for the last time in Tehran, the professor I mentioned at the outset, who takes part in all the protests for Mahsa Amini with a little embarrassment, as he is always the oldest one there.

In 1988, thousands of dissidents were hanged. Among them

were young men and women nationalists and communists who had stormed the American embassy in 1979 alongside Ebtekar; ten years after fighting the Revolution for the ayatollahs, the clerics wanted them dead. A small percentage of them included terrorists responsible for murdering clerics who were members of the institutions of the Islamic Republic. In fact, Supreme Leader Ali Khamenei lost his right hand in one such failed assassination attempt. He has worn a plastic prosthesis ever since.

At the time of the hangings, the head of the judiciary handing down death sentences was Ebrahim Raisi. On the day of the presidential elections in June 2021, the reformists who had supported Masoumeh Ebtekar for the vice-presidency three times over vanished into nothing. From twenty million votes, she received just over two. It was then that Ebrahim Raisi was named president.

Part Two: Ukraine

III.
The First Generation

"Putin will lose the war, but he'll be victorious in depriving a country he hates of its finest citizens: the most intelligent, most generous, and most courageous of us—'the golden generation.'"

A mourner at the funeral
of Roman Ratushnyi, Kyiv, June 18, 2022

In late January 2022, Kateryna, a twenty-eight-year-old woman, took me to a party in an underground club in Kyiv. Later, she took me to a second club, which was connected to the first via a tunnel illuminated with purple lights—but that wasn't the original plan. I had reached out to her for an interview, and she agreed to meet up after dinner. We started by having a drink. When the bartender turned up the volume of the music, I realized that my audio recording of our conversation would be unusable, but it felt like the wrong time and place to pull out my notebook. Never interfere with a local person's plan is a good rule to follow when sent abroad to cover a story. So I didn't take out my pen, I didn't ruin her night.

"The whole world is scared that war is going to break out here," I began by saying. "US intelligence is sure it's going to happen. They even mentioned a date: Wednesday, February 16. What do you think about that?"

"I hope it does."

"You hope war breaks out?" I all but shouted in reply,

in part because the music was so loud and in part because I thought she was delirious.

"Yes, I hope there will be war. We all know that sooner or later there has to be. And I'm not a coward; I wouldn't want to live under constant threat from Vladimir Putin and leave the task of dealing with him to the next generation. Delaying it would be idiotic: it would just extend the agony and hurt Ukraine. It also won't change the monstrosity of what will come next. Of the violence that awaits us."

Gin and tonic in hand, Kateryna communicated what one month later everyone would come to recognize as "the Ukrainian spirit."

"I don't care if it happens tomorrow, in one year, or in five years. I don't want to live under Vladimir Putin's rules, in a world where the truth gets turned upside down. My generation doesn't want that. We don't want it today, we don't want it in a year, and we definitely don't want it five years from now. We've already proven our strength. We've already successfully revolted against Putin, and there aren't many people in the world who can say that. We've managed to change life here, and although I'm not sure how much of that people living elsewhere understand, for us it is a concrete fact. Life under Putin is completely different; we know that, and you do not. We have already made major changes to our lives, and we're not going to give them up."

There's a big difference between saying "I want something" and "I'm not going to give something up." I realized that, if war broke out, the Ukrainians could potentially lose a great deal, but that Putin would never really win. Because winning is not just about occupying land, even for those who consider a country a treasure to be plundered; the inhabitants of a nation are a far more precious commodity than any number of square kilometers.

A few of Kateryna's friends join us. We order Negronis. One

of them has an online fashion company that sells plain T-shirts, sweatshirts, and sweatsuits in pastel colors at unreasonably high prices; he makes most of his money on Instagram. Tall and skinny, his face and hands are covered with tattoos. Another friend works in event planning and brand communication; she's well-dressed and wears only a little make-up.

The oldest of the friends who joins us is a designer from Kharkiv, the second largest city in Ukraine, located in the east. He has a short grey beard and wears chunky rings; he designs and creates masks for Slipknot, an American rap-metal band whose songs get hundreds of millions of clicks on Spotify.

The skinny man with the tattoos started a brand called Papui, which in Ukrainian means "I don't give a fuck." The company hit peak sales during the election campaign that led to Volodymyr Zelensky's victory, when the future president's right-hand man, who was also Zelensky's manager when he was a comedian, appeared alongside him on a television debate in a sweatshirt with the word "Papui" printed across it. Given the setting, the sweatshirt became something of a sensation, much to the delight of the brand's owner.

Many in this group of friends originally met while playing airsoft, a game that involves shooting each other with fake guns in a simulated war. Kateryna has also been a model; she lived in Italy for a time and has friends all across Europe. Her Instagram profile includes photos from a holiday in Ibiza where she rented a house in the same complex as a group of my friends, the same year I graduated from high school. She has a tattoo that is identical to that of a friend of mine from university.

Generally speaking, we empathize more with people who resemble us. A person living in southern Italy is more affected by a case of domestic abuse that happens in a building nearby than by major violence that takes place in Bolzano. This is one of the basic reasons why the war in Ukraine unsettled us Westerners more than the ongoing one in Yemen. Seeing millions of women, children, and elderly flee their homes in North Face jackets, holding cat carriers, shows us what it would be like if a missile were to fall on our own apartment blocks. We're not used to death or desperate enough to consider abandoning our cats, of letting them die of cold or hunger under the bombs. Escaping with a cat in tow symbolizes how normal—and comfortable—their lives were; we would do the same thing, and that makes it even more frightening. Being able to situate certain data (the number of missiles, the number of victims) within a context that we understand leads us to empathize—which is why, for the majority of us, it's easier to relate to what's happening in Kyiv than in Sanaa. With Sanaa, that element of identification that unsettles us simply isn't as powerful.

As with all wars, we knew from the outset that the feeling of solidarity with those being bombed wouldn't last forever. Weariness, boredom, skepticism, and eventually even irritation set in. Our attention and empathy lasted longer than expected, and definitely longer than for other wars, but fatigue and impatience crept in all the same.

Bye-bye Europe

Kateryna belongs to the generation that is deciding the fate of Ukraine, as well as, to some degree, that of Europe. Once Ukraine was under attack, many of us started to feel closer to the country's cause because of the political role that Kyiv assumed in the face of Vladimir Putin and the set of values he represents. Beginning in 2014, and while making some horrific mistakes—war crimes committed by both nationalist militias and separatists at the beginning of the Donbas war—Kyiv has raised its voice to be heard on one basic fact: life is better under the rules of the European Union than under an autocracy that follows Putin's despotic laws. In no uncertain terms, Kyiv has said: we want to cut ties with our Soviet legacy and forge a new bond with you in Europe.

It was a powerful and original voice, although initially not widely heard. In those days, when EU institutions were mentioned, it was because they were being criticized. The generally accepted line of thinking was that liberal democracy was sluggish and flawed, and that, all things considered, Vladimir Putin and Xi Jinping were effective. This was particularly true for the latter, who brought prosperity to the Chinese middle class while that same class in the West was becoming increasingly impoverished. Meanwhile, more EU flags flew in Kyiv than in any city within the Union itself.

Ukrainians saw political Europe as a goal worth fighting and risking their lives for, while people living in its countries joked about the freedoms we have come to take for granted. The political parties that grew the fastest in the polls were those that—to varying degrees—flirted with the "Putin model." They insinuated doubt: things would run more smoothly under the leadership of a strong commander with a straightforward manner, what was needed was a little less rule of law and a little more tradition, a return to less complicated times. Autocracies were seen as somewhat ambiguous, almost sexy, while liberal democracies were always mentioned in tandem with the word "crisis." In this, Kyiv went against the tide.

The political countercurrent was initiated by twenty-year-old Ukrainians. They're the true interpreters of what has since been dubbed "the Ukrainian spirit," which is essentially a combination of grit, irony, and courage.[23] Twenty-year-old Ukrainians are powerful: they're numerous, they managed to change the destiny of their country in the last decade through protest, and they're the ones who are currently fighting the country's war. It's impossible to fully understand what Kyiv is fighting for without getting to know the country's youth.

Twenty-year-old Ukrainians today constitute the first generation to grow up in an independent country: the nation came into being in 1991. Their parents and grandparents, meanwhile, both considered the Soviet Union their home, at least for a time.

This new generation has had a troubled existence. The first person I spoke to about this subject was Mariam Naiem, a twenty-year-old Ukrainian woman of Afghan origin. "Our life has been full of challenges," she told me. "The first challenge we had to face is not one that gets talked about, and it might not even be in the history books, but it made us tough. Our first challenge was survival." When she and her peers were born, the country was in the midst of one of the worst crises of the century. For many years from 1988 onwards, more than half the population had to get by on less than five dollars a day. Unlike the rest of the world in the 1990s, Ukrainian children lived in conditions that were worse than what their parents had experienced.

To help me understand her generation's ambitions and struggles, Naiem told me the much-venerated story of Roman Ratushnyi.

I actually met Roman's mother, Svetlana, and Vasia, one of his friends, in an underground restaurant in Maidan, Kyiv. They wanted to meet there because of the political importance of the Maidan uprising, and because the restaurant, located below street level, had glass display cases that contained gloves, thermoses, and tents that the activists slept in during the protests of 2013 and 2014. There is also a framed print-out of the Facebook post, from the winter of 2013, that announces their first call to action.

Svetlana told me how the 1990s were "hell," how tiring and overwhelming they were, how, without money in their pockets, they could barely rejoice at their hard-won independence. Later, in 2004, she used to take Roman, who was only six at the time, out into the streets of Kyiv with her to take part in the "Orange Revolution" demonstrations. She recalled how they protested the election fraud that had handed victory to the pro-Russian candidate, Viktor Yanukovych. Ten years later, that same Yanukovych was forced to flee to Moscow during the Euromaidan uprising. Then, in early 2022, Yanukovych was transported by military plane to Belarus, at the border with Ukraine, the closest Russian point to the capital. According to the Kremlin's plans (and the Pentagon's predictions), Kyiv would fall in 48-72 hours; Yanukovych needed to be ready to replace Volodymyr Zelensky in a coup d'état. The war was supposed to end immediately. Putin would once again have someone within the presidential palace in Kyiv who would call him before making any decisions.

In 2004, the Orange Revolution, in which Svetlana and Roman took part, won their cause. The Supreme Court called for new elections, and Yanukovych lost. Even so, in 2010 Yanukovych became president of Ukraine.

Adolescence amid the flames

Roman is fifteen when the Euromaidan uprising begins. His face is gaunt, his attitude is aggressive, and the hood of his sweatshirt is always pulled up. Roman stops going to school and sets up camp in the main square of the capital. He's not worried about missing class; he's far ahead of his classmates, he reads a book a week—mainly history—and his teachers refer to him as "the smart black bloc kid." In the square where the Euromaidan protests take place, he earns a reputation for something he says: "The difference between the Russians and us is that when there's a protest in Moscow, the demonstrators run away from the police; when there's a protest in Ukraine, it's the police who run from us." Rarely are there peaceful protests in countries where there's little or no democracy, and Euromaidan was no exception. The police were violent and arrogant, and the demonstrators—at that particular stage—beat up news reporters and politicians who took Putin's side.

Roman joined the people in the square to speak out against

President Yanukovych, who, six months earlier, had deceived his citizens when he announced he would sign a trade agreement with Europe. The goal of the agreement had been to set up an area of free trade with Brussels, but, symbolically, it was more than that. It was a decisive first step towards integration with the European Union, a sign that Roman and all the others wanted to believe. In September 2013, Yanukovych was clear on the matter and told his party members that anyone who did not agree with him on the new European route should abandon ship.

Two months later, while Yanukovych was in Austria, Prime Minister Mykola Azarov announced, to everyone's surprise, that the signing of the agreement had been suspended. The president lacked the courage to communicate it himself, and no details followed. A large number of Ukrainians, who knew perfectly well where this reconsideration came from, and to whom the government truly answered, gathered in Maidan after reading the Facebook post that was later framed and put on display in the underground restaurant. They didn't want to see this window of opportunity close without putting up a fight. The formal announcement came a few days before the summit in Vilnius, Lithuania, where the agreement ought to have been signed and ratified. The conditions set by Europe for Ukraine included the release of Yulia Tymoshenko, the leader of the Orange Revolution, arrested two years earlier. Obviously, the stakes were high, and a figure in the shadows, whose name was never mentioned during the negotiations, was pulling the strings of Yanukovych's actions. Vladimir Putin threatened retaliation if the agreement was signed. It was a clear call to order. At dawn on December 2, 2013, with the Vilnius summit concluded, the pact in shambles, Ukraine slipped away from Europe and back towards Russian control, something its people had been hoping to avoid for the past six months. Thousands of citizens had already taken to the streets in Kyiv to demand that Ukraine sign the agreement in Vilnius. Their voices were ignored—and with that, the Euromaidan uprising began.

Euromaidan was not just a protest against Viktor Yanukovych and Vladimir Putin, it was a protest for something tangible. It was the sound of Ukraine knocking on the door of the European Union. Like any uprising, it not only represented an outburst of collective frustration, it also had a clear objective and a fair chance of success. In fact, it represents Europe's last successful revolution.

Out in the streets, Roman and other activists organize English classes, self-defense workshops, lectures on European history and on the history of protest; they create a civic education initiative open to everyone called the Free University of Maidan. The idea is to create a common culture that looks ahead to the future: "a new community for a new Ukraine." Their main meeting places include public buildings in Kyiv, such as the House of Trade Unions, but the protests spread and even reach the Russian-speaking eastern part of the city. In his *Ukrainian Diaries*, Andrej Kurkov recounts the Euromaidan march on Donetsk that took place on December 30, 2013. At least three hundred people take part; they are followed each step of the way by Russian supporters and plainclothes policemen. That peaceful march is interrupted not by the police, but by groups of elderly ladies who bombard the protesters with rotten eggs from their windows, crying out polite slogans such as, "Long live Russia."

Ten years later, thousands of those same ladies, now a decade older, refused to leave their homes and be evacuated to safety by the Kyiv army. Nothing could convince them to go. They had spent their lives there; some of them had even survived World War II and other disasters. Or maybe it was because the Kyiv army wouldn't let them bring Marta, the cow, or the family-owned pig—"It's all I have"—as was well documented in Bachmut. Or maybe the elderly women simply wouldn't espouse the cause of Euromaidan and the change it set in motion for Ukraine.

In early 2014, President Yanukovych began to fear the protests and the power they were effectively having in the capital. He reacted hastily, forcing Parliament to vote with a show of hands in favor of a series of repressive laws that, among other things, prohibited more than three people from congregating in the street at a time.

The first protester died on January 22, 2014. A twenty-year-old Armenian, Serhiy Nigoyan, was standing at the barricades, reciting poems by the famous Ukrainian poet, Taras Shevchenko. The police shot him; the moment he died represents the tipping point.

The activists occupy a number of city buildings, including the House of Culture, the House of Trade Unions, and the October Palace. They bring their wounded there. In mid-February, the police forcibly regain control of the occupied buildings and shelters by throwing grenades into the House of Trade Unions. The resulting fire kills fifty demonstrators. A few months later, on May 2, neo-Nazi ultras will replicate this tragedy in Odessa, setting fire to that city's House of Trade Unions where forty-two pro-Russian activists sought refuge after taking to the streets, trying to distance themselves from the Maidan movement.

In January 2014, Kyiv is in flames. Tens of thousands of people are out in the streets, the temperature is negative ten degrees Celsius, they have nowhere to take shelter, and they are exposed to firebombs and water cannons. The protesters ask the population for thermoses of hot soup, firewood to burn to stay warm, bottles they could use to make Molotov cocktails, and plastic ponchos to protect themselves from the water cannons. The response is swift and generous. Many of those thermoses now sit in the display cases in museums. After more than a hundred deaths, on February 22, 2014, Yanukovych is forced to sign an agreement with the opposition calling for early elections and a return to the 2004 Constitution. After dismantling the repressive measures, he flees to Russia.

Roman celebrates his sixteenth birthday in the main square. He has won two battles against Yanukovych, which is to say against Vladimir Putin, and heads up a network of peers and activists ready to follow him anywhere. At the time, they didn't know that this would mean being sent to the front lines.

Galvanized, they proudly declaim: "In this day and age, no one knows how to stage a revolution, except us." Eight years later, Putin will punish them for their successes with a full-scale war, which they will have no choice but to fight, and in which many will die.

The most paranoid (and the wisest)

Not even Kyiv could say, in early 2022, whether there would be an invasion or not. Ukrainian authorities kept repeating "panic is a recipe for failure," trying to play down the events, and publicly asking the Americans to stop being so alarmist. Shopkeepers went out and protested against a tax increase of a fraction of a percentage point, which, twenty days later, would seem absurd. I stood at the entrance to nursery school N570 (in Ukraine, as in Russia, schools and hospitals are identified by numbers, a Soviet legacy), located in the suburbs, and stopped at the front gates to talk to mothers and fathers after they dropped off their children, before setting off for work. The school is in a residential neighborhood, surrounded by a cluster of large, twenty-story apartment blocks, a park, and a shopping center. There was half a meter of snow on the ground.

Veronica is a mother of five, and of all the people I talked to, she is the most worried. She has four young children and one eighteen-year-old son, who could be called up at any time; she's concerned for him. Veronica recently started a neighborhood committee to ask the township for an explanation of what is going on. In reply, the town council installs signs in the lobbies of all the buildings indicating the underground shelters that people should use in case of a bombardment. But the shelters are nothing more than basements with few facilities and hardly any reinforcement. "We might be safe there from one missile, but definitely not from two aimed at the same spot."

Veronica stocks up on everything, especially petrol. She's in four different WhatsApp chat groups, one for each of her children's classes. There's always one mother who insists that they should "sew their children's blood type into their kids' smocks." There's also always a mother who accuses the others of being paranoid. There's also always a father who complains that, because of all this talk about war, the country is losing billions of dollars in foreign investments, causing the inflation rate to soar.

Zelensky's approval rating is at an all-time low. At the end of January 2022, only twenty-seven percent of Ukrainians polled say they approve of his government. The president does not convince them. Zelensky is engaged in double discourse: he says things to reassure his country, but he also warns foreign governments about the possibility of an imminent Russian coup. In the meantime, ninety tons of weapons land at Kyiv Boryspil International Airport every day.

In this tense atmosphere, the most paranoid (and the wisest) individuals download a PDF document entitled "In case of emergency or war," with the word "war" written in bold. The document recommends stocking up on canned food and candles, lots of candles, as well as diesel. It suggests taping windows to prevent glass from turning into shrapnel in case of an explosion. And it advises all family members to carry a piece of paper with their blood group on it in their pockets at all times. There are also tips on how to behave in case of shoot-outs or cannon fire: never look at the enemy, turn your head away from the direction of gunshot, stay low down on the ground, keep your mouth open.

A diplomatic advisor to Zelensky once told me: "We expect them to try and sabotage our infrastructure, to hack our systems and intelligence operations; we do not expect a twentieth-century-style invasion." An analyst who works as a consultant for the Ukrainian Foreign Ministry, a thirty-year-old woman, told me the same. When I telephoned her on the morning the invasion began, while I was traveling to Kyiv, she did not reply. She sent me a message: "I can't talk, I'm in a secret location. I'll find you." She was on Putin's list of Ukrainians to be killed immediately, a list that had been distributed to Russian agents who had infiltrated the city months earlier, which specified that the assassinations should begin as soon as tanks crossed the borders. She was a person of influence and had a political following; she had protested on the streets for Euromaidan and, after 2014, became part of the ruling class. Essentially, she had rapidly gone from protest to power, as one does during revolutions.

The only regular person who believed that things would unfold the way they actually did was Kateryna. The only authority figure who did was Kyrylo Budanov. This very young general, who became the head of Ukrainian military intelligence in 2020 at the age of thirty-four, was, at age thirty-six, in charge of organizing the resistance movement in the most serious war in Europe since World War II.

On the evening of February 23, 2022, Budanov does not go home. He sits at his desk in his office. Next to his computer, he has an aquarium, in which he keeps his lucky charm, a pet frog. He's certain that the war will begin soon, and that it will not just focus on the Donbas, in eastern Ukraine, as many people think. He believes that he knows exactly when the invasion will start—on February 24—and at what time—half past four in the morning. On the evening of February 23, he calls his wife, Marianna, and tells her to join him at his office, that they will spend the night there.

The couple met a few months before the beginning of the Euromaidan protests, and were married in 2014; he went off to fight in the war shortly after. Marianna is employed by the city of Kyiv and works as an advisor to Mayor Vitali Klitschko on the fight against corruption. She has been a volunteer at the capital's military hospital for years. Petite, with long black hair and a full mouth, she was the one who removed shrapnel from her husband's body when he was wounded in combat for the second time; in 2019, two Russians placed an explosive device under their car. Marianna is a psychologist by training. When asked how people adapt to the idea that, at any given moment, they might encounter someone who wants to kill them, kidnap them, or sell them to Putin, she replies drily: "On average, human beings can adapt to anything in twenty-one days. I studied that kind of thing at university, but I learned it by living in post-Euromaidan Ukraine."

Kyrylo Budanov and Marianna Budanova were certain that a full-scale invasion would begin soon because they had chosen to trust a man named Denis Kiryeyev. Budanov had done even more than trust him. He had recruited him.

On February 23, Kiryeyev calls Budanov to say that Moscow has made a decision. "They're going to invade." He tells Budanov that the invasion will start at dawn, and that they will enter the capital via Hostomel airport. Dozens of helicopters will be the first to land, carrying the Moscow paratroopers, some of the best men in the Russian armed forces. The men from the Ukrainian special forces, dressed in their combat gear, join Budanov and Marianna Budanova in the large office. They order from McDonald's and eat burgers and fries, their rifles tucked between their boots. They wait. From half past four in the morning and for the next few hours, there is intense communication between Budanov and Volodymyr Zelensky. When the Ukrainian special forces take up position around Hostomel airport, the White House calls Zelensky to ask if he needs help escaping, to save himself. His reply has since become famous: "I need ammunition, not a ride."

It's not easy to find someone in Ukraine who talks at any length about being afraid. This is as true for Kateryna as it is for Budanova or Zelensky. In that moment, in the presidential office, very few people believed that the capital would actually be saved.[24]

Operation Hostomel, which Russian paratroopers hoped would allow them to infiltrate the city center and reach the landmark buildings of democracy, was a suicide mission for Moscow.

The Ukrainians, hiding in bushes and behind airport machinery, ambushed and shot almost all of them. The Russians had hoped to enter and seize the strongholds of democracy in a matter of hours, two days at the most; they thought they'd have the country in hand without a fight. A country's fall or survival depends on how well it defends its capital. While it's impossible to know how things would have turned out without Kiryeyev's tip-off, thanks to his information, Kyiv is still standing, and still free.

Kiryeyev left a promising career in finance in the West, where he worked for Citibank and ING, to do "family banking," managing the assets of two oligarch brothers from Donetsk, owners of important mines in the area. These two oligarchs were friends of the old guard of Ukrainian politicians; in other words, they were pro-Russian. In particular, they were close friends of former president Viktor Yanukovych, who fled to Russia—together with the two brothers and then-head of the SBU (the Ukrainian secret service agency in Kyiv)—during the Euromaidan protests.

Kiryeyev is short and stocky, balding, and fond of cigars. He is known to be friendly, outgoing, and good at building relationships. He speaks Ukrainian, Russian, French, and English. He has a nice house, private bodyguards, and several cars, including one luxury vehicle, and he enjoys spending time at the beach in Greece. He also goes hunting in the Carpathians with the leaders of the SBU. When Russia begins to amass troops at the border the first time around—in the spring of 2021, one year before the full-scale invasion—Budanov summons Kiryeyev and asks him to use his contacts to infiltrate Moscow's military intelligence. Later, he explains why he chose Kiryeyev. "The world of special services and the world of finance are always connected, like the world of crime, at least in our countries."[25]

Kiryeyev has the most useful and dangerous job of all. While staying loyal to Kyiv, he maintains his relationships with the Russians. This means he is unsafe everywhere: defamatory rumors circulate about him in Ukraine, and dangerous ones in Moscow. He can't counter either. He is more precious than a general but doesn't have any of the honor associated with that rank. And what makes things even harder is that Kiryeyev is not from the military; he's not committed to self-sacrifice. He's accustomed to the world of high finance, to personal and immediate reward. When Zelensky was elected in 2019, Kiryeyev was on the shortlist of candidates to head Ukraine's most important publicly controlled bank. He held all the right cards for the appointment but was denied the possibility because of a press campaign against him. Journalists who were understandably ill-informed about the work of an undercover agent perceived him as having Russian connections.

On the evening of February 18, 2022, six days before the invasion, Kiryeyev goes home to his wife and son and tells them, at dinner, that he can't join them the following day on a ski trip they had planned to the French Alps. On February 23, he calls Budanov and says, "Vladimir Putin will give the order to invade early tomorrow morning." He then goes on to share all the technical details of the planned attack at Hostomel airport.

Budanov later said that, thanks to Kiryeyev's tip, Ukraine gained a precious few hours to shift troops and was able to counter the Russian assault.[26]

The war begins. Kiryeyev is part of the Ukrainian delegation that meets in Belarus with the Moscow delegation to try—unsuccessfully—to block the invasion. Present at these meetings was also the Russian multi-billionaire and former owner of Chelsea FC, Roman Abramovich. Shortly after one of their meetings, Abramovich starts to show symptoms of being poisoned. Kiryeyev would have preferred to remain in the background, but Budanov and Zelensky had asked him to go.

Moscow is obsessed with the Hostomel fiasco; they can't figure out how that critical maneuver for Russia turned into a massacre of their best men. They want to know who warned Kyiv. Seeing Kiryeyev at the meetings on behalf of the Ukrainian delegation may have led Moscow to start asking questions about the level of his involvement. Perhaps they had other reasons for suspecting him. They could easily have gotten their revenge on him by poisoning him at one of those meetings.

Kiryeyev didn't even tell his wife that he'd be attending the summit in Belarus. She would have surely stopped him from going. But Kiryeyev was not poisoned by the Russians. He was killed in Kyiv by the men who were supposed to be protecting him: SBU agents, the Ukrainian secret service. An SBU official later stated that Kiryeyev died because he was spying for Putin. This was false. "If it hadn't been for Kiryeyev, Kyiv would have probably been taken by the Russians," Budanov says. Zelensky decorated him posthumously with a medal of honor "for his extraordinary sacrifice in defense of Ukraine." Kiryeyev was given a state funeral worthy of a national hero.

In July, Zelensky fired the head of the SBU. Kiryeyev was not a spy; his killers were.

In Ukraine, more than six hundred trials for treason involving public officials are on the docket. Many of them revolve around members of the secret service.

I was in Kyiv on the day Kiryeyev, the man who saved the city, was found on the sidewalk with a bullet hole at the base of his skull. I would return to Kyiv numerous times after those early days of war, and it was always lively, bustling with people, and filled with flowers. But in March 2022, it was just plain frightening.

I arrived at the station during curfew. I stepped out of the pedestrian underpass with my hands raised, holding a white flag that I had fashioned out of a bidet towel stolen for this precise purpose from a hotel in the city of Khmelnytskyi. Everything in Kyiv was closed and shuttered. The authorities had said that anyone found wandering in the streets would be suspected of being a Russian saboteur. Air raid sirens blared. The precise and powerful anti-aircraft artillery from the West had not yet arrived; Russian missiles reached their targets. I was walking down an empty road when a soldier pointed his rifle at me, asked for identification, and told me to open my bag. His inspection went on until two bombs exploded nearby. We looked at each other tacitly (he didn't speak English and I don't speak Ukrainian) and realized that we both had more urgent things to do—in my case, find shelter.

I knocked on doors, but no one opened up for me. I rushed after a man who was racing into a bunker and called out to him to wait, but he shut the door in my face. I made it to one of the few hotels in the city that was still open and had guests. The next day, a girl who worked as a waitress whispered, "I shouldn't be telling you this, but you're not safe here." What she meant was that if the Russians surrounded the city, they'd shut down the hotel, and people like her would rush off to their mothers and children. I could easily be chased out during a siege or while there was fighting in the street, with no food or bunker. A man wandered through the lobby offering people rides in his van, "no questions asked." On the first day, a seat in the vehicle cost three thousand euros. On the second day, the price went up to ten thousand. "We're running out of food. We're definitely not going to spend money stocking up for customers now," the waitress said.

I walked around with a large plastic bag and a backpack that held a knife, some vacuum-packed cheese and salami, a powerful power bank, some cash, breadsticks, lots of cigarettes, and a small bottle of whisky. Alcohol had been banned and confiscated: people needed to be ready to fight, the government did not want to deal with zombies who'd drunk away their fear. Gas stations were closed because they'd run out of fuel: people had filled their jerry cans before fleeing to Poland or Hungary, or to keep at home, just in case. The army had requisitioned some, too.

No one was entirely sure if the capital would be safe. The Russians could still capture it. Elderly women patrolled the streets looking for Russian spies; a general state of paranoia hovered in the air; Ukrainians saw Putin's saboteurs everywhere. Some of the people who were arrested, such as looters, were tied to poles with tape and stripped naked. In the neighborhood of Podil, someone set fire to a car and bus where alleged infiltrators were sleeping, the charred bodies remaining there for all to see. You had to have your passport in hand at all times: if the armed Ukrainian civilians who manned the roadblocks suspected you of being Russian, and you had to reach into your coat or bag to take out your passport, they might think you were taking out a weapon, not a document, and shoot you on the spot.

From activists to soldiers

I spent several days in the fields on the outskirts of the city, where people from all walks of life were training for combat. Retired women and unemployed people maneuver fake rifles; a Porsche Cayenne owned by a well-known businessman is parked nearby; there's also a publisher, his two printer friends, high school students, and a kindergarten teacher.

I had already met the teacher, Natalye, outside N570. She's thirty-six, but with her long painted nails and fake eyelashes, she looks much younger. She has a fourteen-year-old daughter and has been teaching at N570 for twelve years. Like everyone else, her life changed at the end of 2013. She followed the Maidan protests but with a young child and a job, she couldn't actively participate in them. And yet, on the most dangerous day of fighting, when snipers fired live rounds at eye-level, she rushed in with bandages, syringes, and painkillers. Corpses lay on the ground for hours, and only later were lined up under the small white and gold gate that looks out on the square. To flush out the protesters who had occupied a Western Union building, the police threw grenades, which led to more fatalities: people were burned to death or died from smoke inhalation. From that point on, every day after leaving work at the nursery school, Natalye delivered sleeping bags and thermoses full of borscht to the square. A few months later, in 2014, when fighting began in Donbas, Natalye started travelling by car to the front, bringing the soldiers everything they could possibly need, including underwear. When she got there, she'd empty the packed car and hang drawings made by the children for the soldiers on the walls of their trenches.

When Putin started preparing for the full-scale invasion, Natalye changed gears; she was no longer satisfied with just lending a hand. The training camp where she learns to do battle is located in a forest sixty kilometers south of Kyiv, towards Odessa. Her battalion is called Marussia's Bears, with Marussia their forty-year-old leader, a war veteran who was a paratrooper in Donbas. Marussia not only teaches them how to shoot, but also how to survive in icy water; they scramble through narrow tunnels made of tires while fellow soldiers throw firecrackers at them to simulate trench warfare. There are many such groups scattered around the country. The most recent people to enlist include a priest, a beautician, and a teenager who told me that learning to defend himself cured his insomnia, that he could finally sleep at night.

Fortunately for these civilians, and for Kyiv, no one has seriously considered sending them to the front. Ukrainian doctrine tries to emulate—as much as possible—NATO countries. War is a job for professionals who need to rely on special units and technology, who prefer traps and ambushes to frontal assaults in open fields, who opt for surprise attacks that force the enemy to flee or retreat (as in the counteroffensive attack in the Kharkiv region in September 2022, or in Kherson in November 2022) rather than attritional attack strategies, which would mean numerous deaths (as in all the assaults in Donbas). Professional soldiers prefer surgical strikes—against strategic hubs like warehouses, arms depots, and command centers, making it impossible for the enemy to hold their positions—to widespread, indiscriminate bombing. Moscow's technique is the latter.

Russia mainly relies on two things: the production of millions of artillery shells—basic, cheap, and without integrated technology, which ultimately do more damage because they strike chaotically, hitting a wide area instead of a specific target—and hundreds of thousands of often inexperienced and almost always poorly equipped soldiers. Before invading Ukraine, Putin reinstated a bonus that had initially been created by Stalin during the war with Hitler: one million rubles to every Russian mother who "produced" ten children or more. Ten months into the conflict, Yevgeny Prigozhin's Wagner mercenary company, which recruited men and women to be sent to Ukraine from Russian prisons, had to begin imposing basic rules for selection: you had to be able to do a hundred squats without losing your balance and falling over. In fact, during the first ten months of the war, he sent so many pathologically ill alcoholics to the trenches that some died after only a week in Donbas, before even firing a shot.

Natalye and her comrades did not end up at the front, but the vast and spontaneous mobilization of Ukrainian civilians at the outset of the war sent a powerful message not only to the Russians and the West, but to their own government. It provided the context that allowed Zelensky to firmly pronounce the words that have ended up on mugs and T-shirts: "I need ammunition, not a ride." Those hundreds of hours of training—which, like all military training, went far beyond learning how to load a weapon—instructed the Ukrainian people what kinds of material to use for shelter during a bombardment and which to avoid, how to stop external bleeding, and how to resuscitate a person who had fallen to the ground.

The civilians who went to battle included athletes, young and healthy individuals, people with specific skills that were useful to the military, people who had been training for months or years, and, most of all, people who knew exactly which side of the war they were on. Kateryna, at twenty-eight, and Roman, at twenty-three, both volunteered and became part of the army.

When the invasion began, Roman was already famous in Kyiv. He was never naïve, even at an age when it's generally acceptable to be. He understood that it wasn't enough for Yanukovych to flee Ukraine for there to be change. The country had other problems that needed to be tackled: endemic corruption, oligarchs, an unreliable judicial system, violent law enforcement agencies that used mobster methods, and the presence of Putin's spies within the state institutions.

Roman is an environmental activist and is against police violence. He organizes protests as well as acts of sabotage; he's a political figure with a significant following. The authorities don't like him. At a certain point, he even has a violent confrontation with a member of Zelensky's cabinet.

Roman and Julija establish an association they call "Save Protasiv Yar." Both of them grew up in the neighborhood of Protasiv Yar, which includes a forest, the largest green space in Kyiv. A group of builders—and some oligarchs with criminal connections—want to build blocks of forty-story buildings in Protasiv Yar. Roman takes the construction companies to court, but things proceed neither smoothly nor swiftly, so he and his followers start to destroy the building site with sledgehammers. It would appear that "the smart black bloc kid" hasn't changed much. When Julija spoke to me, she referred to him as "an intelligent troublemaker." Roman toes the line between legal and illegal, and even crosses it sometimes, but he usually manages to avoid serious trouble. This is partly because he is skilled with words, and partly because he studied law for this very purpose. He wanted "to learn how to argue for a good cause." Roman, Julija, and the others occupy the construction site and block the entrances. After two years of protests, in 2021, Roman wins: Protasiv Yar is declared a protected natural area, and a formal ban on building is imposed. But during those two years, Roman has made many enemies. Although he's not the type to be easily frightened, he begins to receive death threats that include details about his private life and personal movements. He decides to disappear for a while. He doesn't consider asking the police for protection because he knows they don't like him.

Between 2010 and 2013, after the killing of Igor Indylo—a twenty-year-old student who died in a case not unlike that of George Floyd—a movement against police violence emerged in Ukraine. Roman and Kateryna Handziuk, old comrades-in-arms, were part of this movement. In 2018, Kateryna was chosen by the mayor of Kherson, her hometown, to become a city council member. She sustained a brutal sulfuric acid attack on July 31 while investigating cases of corruption in the local police force for the mayor. The corrosive liquid reached her internal organs, and she died in the hospital after three months of agony. When Roman first started receiving death threats, a total of fifty-five serious unresolved crimes had been committed against young activists in Ukraine. After seeing the investigation into Kateryna's death get hurried through the courts, Roman joined with others to start a new campaign called "Silence Kills." It worked: the head of the Kherson regional council was arrested for ordering the murder of Kateryna Handziuk, and a number of police officers have since been questioned.

Like Kateryna, Roman—with regards to the Protasiv Yar issue—had also received threats from powerful figures of authority. He does not trust several Ukrainian institutions, but—thanks to the visibility he gained within the EU for his loyalty and dedication to the Euromaidan cause—when he has a problem, he calls Brussels.

Roman had already become the spokesperson for the lawsuit against the Ukrainian police for violence they committed during the Maidan uprising, which was brought before the European Court. He also brought the Protasiv Yar case to the commission set up expressly by the European Union for Ukraine, which was headed by Peter Wagner. A German national, Wagner got his university degree in Vienna and has worked for European institutions his whole life. When the full-scale invasion of Ukraine began, he was the director of a branch of the Commission that deals with European foreign policy tools. A true EU bureaucrat, he's the kind of person no one bothers writing about—unless they make a mistake, trip up, or end up in a real or alleged scandal. Julija told me how Roman telephoned Wagner, and how she and Roman traveled to Brussels to meet with him. They explained the situation, showed him evidence of the threats, and proved that they came from figures within government institutions. They asked for a show of support. After their meeting, and following a number of private phone calls and public tweets by Wagner, Roman was able to come out of hiding. No one dared threaten him anymore. At the age of twenty-three, he could finally enjoy his most recent hard-won victories and a bit of calm. But only for a few months. Until February 24, 2022.

Roman, his friends, and his mother Svetlana were not fans of Zelensky. They described him to me as "lightweight," "ignorant," "lacking in history," "empty," and even "cowardly." But, they added, that was before the war began. Before the invasion, in the broader Ukrainian political landscape, Zelensky's stance on Putin's Russia was considered ambiguous. For example, on New Year's Eve of 2013, after Euromaidan had already begun, he participated as a comic in a television program hosted by one of Putin's most famous propagandists, Vladimir Solovyov. To this day, Solovyov compares Moscow's war of aggression on Ukraine to the act of deworming a cat, where: "for the doctor (Putin), it's a special operation, for the worms (the Ukrainians), it's a war, and for the cat (Ukraine), it's a cleansing."[27] Svetlana believes, though she has no evidence to support it, that one of the key figures in Zelensky's cabinet is actually a Russian spy.

Among the twenty-year-olds I met in Ukraine, it's hard to find someone who isn't more radical than Zelensky on the issue of how to deal with Russia and Vladimir Putin. Mykhailo Poliakov, another activist and university researcher, says that until the election campaign, "it seemed absolutely impossible that Zelensky would win." From inside his bubble, Mykhailo presumptuously thought that "Someone who makes jokes too banal to be funny, the star of a television series that portrays a populist utopia that no one really believes in" did not stand a chance. "Then, when I realized that he might actually be elected, I was terrified," he says, because Zelensky had shown that he knew next to nothing about the history of Ukraine and its relationship with Moscow. He downplayed the war that had been going on since 2014, saying that "to end it, we just need to stop shooting," and that, in his opinion, all he needed to do was "talk to Putin, look him squarely in the eye" for there to be peace. Mykhailo saw Zelensky as a megalomaniac—until the invasion. Mykhailo and Roman were not alone: the majority of the generation of Ukrainians who initiated the battle against Putin in 2013 did not cast their ballots for Zelensky.

As often happens in a country under siege, old grudges fade fast. On February 24, 2022, the Ukrainian authorities asked Roman for help, and he was eager to provide it. He formed a brigade of volunteers named after his neighborhood and the forest that he saved, Protasiv Yar. Roman is precious to the government for several reasons: he's used to fighting, his loyalty to the cause is well proven, and he has been aware of Russian infiltration in Ukraine for years—for example, he knows all about the oligarchs who continued to work for Putin after 2014, having had personal and dangerous dealings with them. Also, he is not a solo figure but the leader of a group of activists who share a belief system; together they make up a well-oiled military unit with a hierarchy, clear roles, and a strong team spirit. Trust and solidarity cannot be created out of nothing, and building them up had been part of their training period. When war broke out, the Protasiv Yar brigade was ready.

The absence of team spirit within the Russian troops of conscripts deployed in Ukraine in late 2022 represents perhaps the most serious intangible mistake of the Moscow army. When Russian men of military age were forcibly taken from their homes, universities, offices, and even from the hotels where they were on holiday, there simply weren't enough bulletproof vests, helmets, tourniquets, or combat boots to go around. When the army instructed them to procure their own, the prices of these items in Russia soared, and they soon became impossible to find. In the barracks where the conscripts were taken, and in the training camps, those who hadn't been able to afford these items, or who hadn't bought them before they ran out of stock, stole from their comrades. As a result, there were fights, injuries, at least one death, and retaliatory raids. Soldiers forced to steal boots from each other before they get to know one another will have a hard time building team spirit in their unit. And on the front, the less cohesive a unit is, the more soldiers will die.

Meanwhile, in Ukraine, the first task entrusted to the Protasiv Yar brigade was to locate and then ambush and capture Viktor Medvedchuk, an oligarch and friend of Putin, allegedly involved in a plan to oust Zelensky and set up a new, pro-Russian government in Kyiv. Roman has long considered Medvedchuk an enemy; the operation goes smoothly, and Protasiv Yar's efforts lead to his arrest. As Putin's friend, the oligarch was later used in a prisoner exchange, which allowed the Mariupol resistance fighters—the Azov soldiers who had barricaded themselves in the basement of the steelworks—to be released and returned to Ukraine.

A few days after the arrest of Medvedchuk, Roman left with the 93rd Mechanized Brigade of the Ukrainian army for Izjum, in the Kharkiv region, where the fighting was among the most violent, together with that going on in Mariupol. His mission was to fly military drones.

Roman Ratushnyi died in combat in Izjum in the summer of 2022. He was twenty-four years old. I attended his funeral at St. Michael's Cathedral in Kyiv; the church was so crowded you couldn't even move your arms. Kateryna was there. So was Mariam Naiem, the thirty-year-old analyst on Putin's list of Ukrainians to be killed immediately. Naturally, Svetlana, Vasia, and Julija were there, too. An older lady standing next to me said, "Putin will lose the war, but will be victorious in depriving a country he hates of its finest citizens: the most intelligent, most generous, and most courageous of us—'the golden generation.' Their generation is much stronger than mine; we've been sad for a long time, and our sadness has drained us. Now I wish we could die in order to save them."

"My name is Ivan and I am a resistance fighter"

The army is not the only option for people like Kateryna and Roman, who, like many other Ukranians of their generation, are determined never to return to life under Putin's rule. One group of people for whom this is particularly true is the Ukrainian LGBTQ+ community. In the typical rhetoric of the Russian president, one of the aims of their war of aggression is "to protect our children" from Western "degradation and degeneration."[28] Putin has entrusted the moral aspects of his military aggression to Vladimir Mikhailovich Gundyayev, a former KGB agent (the two men were in the secret service together), and to Patriarch Kirill, the Orthodox Christian Patriarch of Moscow and Russia. Kirill believes that the war in Ukraine is a war against the "gay lobby." He sees killing Ukrainians not as a sin, but as an assurance of entry into heaven.

In this context, LGBTQ+ activists could rely on a strong, pre-existing network made up of various groups and associations; they also had stronger motives than others to fear life under occupation. For those who had committed their lives to defending queer rights, when Russia started to amass tanks at the borders, they were concerned about one thing only: how thousands of gay, bisexual, and transgender people would survive in Putin's world.

During wartime, danger takes on many forms. It's not just the bombs being dropped by the Russians on places they have yet to conquer—it's the forced assimilation of people in cities that they have managed to take over. Russian offensives and Ukrainian counteroffensives do not merely occupy or free pieces of land and resources: first and foremost, they occupy and free people.

A number of activists from the LGBTQ+ community had approached the young General Kyrylo Budanov before the beginning of the war, as soon as danger was perceived. General Budanov was also in charge of the pseudo-fascists of the Azov battalion. "Given the circumstances, we weren't worried about Azov. We were worried about Putin," Ivan Shestopalov, a leader of the Ukrainian LGBTQ+ community in Kherson, told me.

Budanov's men trained activists, like Ivan, in guerrilla warfare, how to conceal their pasts, and how to live incognito. After February 24, 2022, some of these activists found themselves living under occupation.

In early November 2022, I traveled to Kherson, in southeastern Ukraine. The Russians had conquered the city in a matter of days. Actually, "conquered" is the wrong word because, basically, Kherson had been abandoned.

The Russians arrived immediately. By March 3, a week into the invasion, they had already occupied everything without having to destroy anything, without even fighting. The soldiers who were supposed to protect the city had either fled or done worse. General Serhiy Kryvoruchko, the head of the local SBU, left before the enemy arrived and ordered his men to do the same. His subordinate, Colonel Ihor Sadokhin, head of the city's anti-terrorist unit, informed the Russians who approached from the south—from Crimea—precisely where they should not set foot, drive their vehicles, or deploy their tanks, because the Ukrainian army had placed mines there. Kyiv's plan, in the event of an attack, had been to blow up the bridges that led to Kherson from Crimea. But the Antonivs'kyi Bridge did not explode, nor did the bridge to the east that crosses the Nova Kachovka dam. It was the inhabitants of Kherson who fought back: they marched in unison with smartphones in their hands—live-streaming on Instagram or TikTok—and forced a column of Russian armored vehicles to retreat. They went on to attack the soldiers in the main square and waved their Ukrainian flags while riding on Russian tanks. The people who ought to have been protecting them had run off, leaving the table set for the invaders.

We know that, at the outset of the war, a number of undercover agents from Moscow were already in Ukraine, studying the territory and the enemy, waiting for orders. But the most insidious were not the spies who had just arrived, but those who had been there for a long time, who held positions in the government. People who, after 2014, pretended to embrace the new political path but secretly never stopped working for Vladimir Putin. When Volodymyr Zelensky fired Attorney General Iryna Venediktova and the head of the secret service, Ivan Bakanov, the event was seen by many as "Zelensky's purges." But calling them "purges" was hasty. The Ukrainian institutions could not defend themselves from Putin if his spies still worked from within. Zelensky did not fire Iryna Venediktova because he did not trust her or her abilities as a magistrate, but because she failed to control her subordinates and what was going on around her. Her office was rife with informers. Bakanov was a childhood friend of Zelensky's. They had worked together at Kvartal 95 Studio, the company that organized Zelensky's comedy shows and which, later, produced his television series. The name they chose for the company was driven by nostalgia, a reference to the 95th district of Kryvyi Rih, where Bakanov and Zelensky grew up. It was not an easy decision for Zelensky to make, and he hesitated for weeks before writing the decree that removed Venediktova and Bakanov from their positions.

The SBU stems from the KGB. As far as secret services go, it is oversized (with thirty thousand employees, it is seven times the size of its British counterpart) and infamous for its corruption and for the presence of double agents long before the invasion began. Its employees were used to working with Russians and for Russia; they'd been doing so their entire lives. It was difficult to eradicate the shadows of the past—because everyone had a Soviet past, they had all been loyal to Putin—but it wouldn't have been possible (or fair) to fire them all. Reforming the institution and rooting out all its internal enemies was not an easy task for Bakanov, but a necessary one. He failed and, consequently, Zelensky gave him the boot. Mistakes made by other leaders, together with the fact that only General Budanov had accurately predicted the methods and timing of the invasion, made the head of military intelligence a very powerful man, perhaps even the most powerful man in the war.

On November 9, 2022, the Russians were forced to withdraw from Kherson. I reached the city by car and spent the afternoon with Ivan Shestopalov, one of the leaders of Inshi, which in Ukrainian means "others," the most important local LGBTQ+ association. Ivan is a gay Ukrainian, and the SBU of Kherson informed Putin about him. Ivan is also a resistance fighter, one of the many activists who asked Budanov's Ukrainian intelligence corps to teach them how to fight. The reasons for his involvement in the war are clear: the prospect of life in a state with homophobic laws does not appeal to him. Ivan has a life partner in the most complete sense of the word: they fight for queer rights together and in armed combat together. His name is Oleksyj and he is twenty-three years old.

In May 2022, with Kherson under occupation, the Russians take Oleksyj captive in the midst of preparing a "violent" act of resistance, the details of which Ivan prefers not to reveal to me. Oleksyj disappears. Ivan fears for him, and for what he might reveal about the association, especially the resistance network. Oleksyj is being held nearby, but underground, in a torture chamber set up in the basement of a former barracks, with chains on his feet. He's kept in the dark for two months. The hammering on his stomach is far more painful than the whipping he receives.

A few days after Oleksyj's arrest, the Russians break into Inshi's office in Kherson, which the activists had hastily sealed up and abandoned. They break the padlocks, pull up the security gates, and empty out the cupboards. They're looking for the registers that contain the names of the association members. They find them, together with their addresses. Some of them have a check mark next to them, those who have already paid their annual dues for 2022. They knock on doors, interrogate people, beat up some of them, and make others disappear. Ivan and the other members of Inshi believe that Oleksyj talked; they believe he ratted them out to stop the torture.

The Russians, after capturing Oleksyj for his Kyiv-coordinated role in the resistance, presumed that other members of Inshi were also involved. While not all activists are resistance fighters, Ivan is. His fear was greater than that of his fellow Inshi members, but he can't talk about it with them. Oleksyj resurfaces in July, disfigured and puffy. He is considered an outcast by the LGBTQ+ community, and his partner has to stop the others from beating him up. One girl calls him a "traitor," saying, "Did you want to get us all killed?" Ivan knows that Oleksyj did not betray them, at least not completely; he knows that he must have revealed something to the Russians, but that he never would have given up the resistance fighters, as they would have been killed. Despite the monstrous effect that war has on people, Ivan can't forget that Oleksyj is only in his twenties, that he is "unhappier than me because braver," and that he spent eight weeks chained up in the dark, getting regularly beaten. Ivan is one of the few who know the truth; almost everyone else thinks Oleksyj is a collaborator. Two people say they want to kill him, "but they never really meant it." Oleksyj listens to the accusations in silence: he has not been broken, he wants to continue to fight. The version he gave the Russians is that he had switched sides, and he needs to stick to that story, even with the people whose affection he'd like to win back. Ivan and Oleksyj stop seeing each other: Ivan doesn't want to be seen as a traitor, and Oleksyj doesn't want Putin's soldiers to become suspicious.

The two men find themselves in the same situation again in September: this time, they both decide to collaborate with the occupiers. The Russians need people to run the city's schools, hospitals, post offices, and sewers. Ivan and Oleksyj volunteer to be postmen, a relatively easy task. Without conferring with each other, both resistance fighters chose a job that granted them freedom of movement in a city where there was none. Kherson was divided into sections and separated by checkpoints that were difficult to cross without a permit—one of the ways the Russians hoped to better control a rebellious population. Postmen, though, can go anywhere on their bikes, and they can gather lots of information: where the Russian soldiers are, which direction they're moving, where the collaborators sleep, and where the weapons are stockpiled. All precious information for the Ukrainian army. The fact that the two resistance fighters, who were not talking to each other for their own safety, had adopted the same tactic at the same time led me to suspect that their moves had been coordinated from an external source in Kyiv—Budanov.

After the Russians withdrew from Kherson, Oleksyj was moved to an undisclosed location in the still-occupied territories. He is among the sixty thousand civilians that the Russian General Sergei Surovikin ordered to be evacuated. He can still prove to be useful.

The useful idiot

The puppet master behind the pro-Russian network that governed Kherson, which Oleksyj first, and then more discreetly, Ivan, infiltrated, was Kirill Stremousov. A tragicomic character who had long interested me, Stremousov was killed a few days before I arrived in Kherson. I had been trying to approach him for weeks through a female friend of his, texting her at length. She had promised to procure an interview with Stremousov for me. When he was killed, she disappeared. Her phone number is no longer in service.

Stremousov first came into the public eye in 2017 as the protagonist of a disturbing video that went viral. In it, a man in his late thirties with brown hair and blue eyes holds his four-month-old daughter upside down, by her feet, and spins her around as if she were a rag doll. Naturally, the child is screaming. "Listen! Listen to the sound of her bones cracking!" the man says. The video was watched by millions but, at the time, its protagonist was essentially unknown. Stremousov's rise in the media started with this stunt and ended with his appointment as the number two figure in the administration of Russian-occupied Kherson.

Stremousov first comes to Kherson in 2009. Initially, according to people who knew him, he is relatively normal. A small business owner, he has a company that makes fish food. When inspectors find fault with his products, the fines are so heavy they threaten the business; he gets ahead of it by quitting his job and reinvents himself by opening a kind of news agency, using it as a front to advertise a shady side business he runs on his social media channels. Basically, by touting the benefits—discounts, tax relief incentives, and so on—available to anyone who belongs to the protected category of journalists, he gets people to register as reporters. He then hands out journalist identification cards as a tool for tax evasion and takes a cut from his fake journalist customers. Predictably enough, he's soon in trouble with the law again. He's stripped of his license, loses his job, takes a trip to the United States, and comes back an entirely different person, amazed by what he has seen. He tells everyone about the people he met while in America, people who told him things that seemed insane at first, but which then revealed a whole new world to him. While in the States, Stremousov spent time with white supremacists, cults, and conspiracy theorists. The "new world" is QAnon.

Stremousov returns to Europe convinced that Vladimir Putin is the savior of a very sick planet Earth. He records a delusional and emotional video on TikTok, where he recites a poem, his eyes glazed over, about his love for the Russian Federation.

The vision that he brings back from the United States is a blend of QAnon theories and the opinions of Aleksandr Dugin, the Slavophile philosopher who is periodically favored by the Kremlin and much loved by Steve Bannon, Donald Trump's former advisor.

As the keeper of a new truth and heavily steeped in a particular brand of esoteric nonsense, Stremousov decides to start his own religion in Ukraine, where one of the commandments is not to pay your taxes. In 2013, at the beginning of the Euromaidan movement, Stremousov and his followers carry a Russian flag into the central square of Kherson. He becomes affiliated with the city's pro-Russian socialist party. He and his followers reject state authority generally, and Ukrainian authority in particular.

The pandemic boosts his rise in popularity from influencer to politician to cult leader. His forceful anti-vax opinions make Stremousov a central source of anti-scientific views on vaccines in the Slavic world and beyond. It is this popularity that the Russians exploit when they arrive in Kherson. When they name him second in command in the administration, he is overjoyed; the Russians are pleased, too, because they need someone expendable who is also easy to manipulate. His role is purely media. He's the face of the occupation, responsible for announcing important events to the people, such as the annexation of Kherson to Russia after the sham referendum in September, the same one where soldiers forced people to vote by showing up at their doors or in building courtyards, armed with rifles.

Being the face of the occupation in a city that is also the headquarters of the Ukrainian resistance fighters means being in constant danger, but Stremousov is galvanized by his mission; he plays along willingly, he's a narcissist. In his last public appearance, he announces the evacuation of civilians to other occupied areas further east, and to territories within the Russian Federation—evacuations in which resistance fighter Oleksyj is also included. A few hours before the announcement that Russian soldiers are beating a retreat, Stremousov dies in a bizarre accident: the car in which he was travelling is riddled with bullets. One hypothesis suggests that he was killed—like other collaborators had been—by the resistance fighters of Kherson. Another possibility is that he was killed by the Russians. He wouldn't have been the first; a number of pro-Russian figures in the Donbas who favored Moscow were killed, either because they made mistakes or as scapegoats for local military failures. For those who stand with Putin but are ineffective at their jobs, death is just one of the ways they can be punished.

Kyiv resistance fighters operate in many different ways; it depends on what they know how to do and what they have the courage to do. Ukraine is one of the most fully digitalized countries in Europe, with countless young people working in the tech sector. I met a young man named Vova who never went to university but who works as a programmer in the cryptocurrency industry. He has long hair and two facial piercings. His apartment is filled with glass bottles that he has been saving for months to use, when the occasion arises, as Molotov cocktails and throw at the vulnerable areas of Russian tanks from his windows. His nom de guerre is VVK@, and his second job is that of cyber-resistance fighter involved in a virtual war against Moscow. Vova is part of Zion, a hacker collective that takes its name from the city of the rebels in *The Matrix*. The collective's leader is safely ensconced in an apartment in Paris, "because with a government in exile, our war can continue no matter what happens here, even if the Russians destroy our internet connection with bombs, like they did in Mariupol, or if Elon Musk decides to take away our Starlink satellites."

Vova does battle on multiple fronts: the first, and most basic, level is via cyberattacks on Russian websites, including those belonging to the government and central bank, and on social media sites, such as VKontakte. Zion has also launched a smartphone app that allows anyone, even those with the most rudimentary technological skills, to participate in mini cyber-attacks against Russian sites. The app is called Digital Cotton. Its creators say it is simple to use, runs on Android, and does not overload phones. "It's a way of making virtual warfare against Russia a mass phenomenon in Ukraine."

Vova also works on a second, more ambitious front: "to get inside the heads of the Russians," he says, sounding much like the dystopian graphic novels that he reads. In practice, Zion hacks into the poorly protected branches of the Russian Defense system—those containing data related to military pension contributions, for example—and steals personal identification information. One of the most useful pieces of data they seek to obtain is the identity of Russians fighting in Ukraine. Zion's system then cross-references this data and tracks down their girlfriends, parents, wives, and even the children of the soldiers, going on to bombard them with images of the dead and mutilated filmed by Kyiv's military drones on the front lines where their relatives were deployed. Numerous videos of this kind exist on the web; they're easy enough to find. More Russian soldiers were killed during the first two weeks of the Ukraine war than American soldiers in twenty years in Afghanistan. Moscow never officially mentions its losses, and the government forbids civilians and journalists from talking about them. "We fill a void," the hackers of Zion say. And they fill it with brutal counter-information.

Vova gave me access to a secure chat room so I could better understand how it works. Access lasts twenty-four hours, after which your credentials expire. When I entered the room, hackers had recently stolen personal information belonging to Russian officers and pilots from the 55th helicopter regiment. They found out names, ages, salaries, schools attended, marital status, and the names of their closest relatives. Their strategy is to start with the mothers of the youngest and poorest soldiers. According to Zion, a person's salary level is "even more important than age," and is a key to finding vulnerable profiles, with spouses who are most likely to get angry. The aim is clear: spread panic and encourage desertion. "They bring their bombs and tanks to Ukraine; we bring a more contemporary war to Russia, one without bloodshed, a war of nerves."

"*The war started long before you realized it*"

A hypothesis exists that can be neither verified nor disproved because it is entirely counterfactual: if we hadn't allowed Vladimir Putin to do what he did in 2014, he wouldn't have invaded Ukraine in 2022. He wouldn't have thought success was possible. The sanctions of 2014 were merely cosmetic.

In the months leading up to the invasion, many of us believed the Russian president would never order his army to cross the borders. Although we did not rule out that Putin was capable of making violent decisions, it seemed far too irrational, even for him. Putin was a powerful man; he had many admirers, even in the West, and he went unchallenged. No one—before the invasion—ever thought there could be a regime change in the Kremlin. However, since the war started, or rather, since things on the battlefield started going worse than expected for Moscow, there has been talk of his possible succession. There has also been talk of how Putin has been embarrassed, of his silences, of the hundreds of thousands of citizens who fled at the beginning of the full-scale invasion and during the early weeks of mobilization.

It's not important whether Putin will be replaced in the near future or not. What is important is that we're talking about it. Putin is significantly weaker today than he appeared to be on February 23, 2022. He has been exposed. In the early 2000s, Anna Politkovskaya wrote that the Russian army was weak and penetrable, while Putin claimed it was powerful and frightening.

We believed Putin. He sought to project himself as powerful, and he was careful about not being "found out." Putin started the war in Ukraine to revive the notion of empire in the country he governs, when in actual fact, Russia was considered a greater power before its tanks crossed the Ukrainian border. Prior to Moscow's disastrous—in terms of expectations—military performance, nobody would have ever associated the word "weak" with Putin's Russia. Nobody ever dreamed that the president of Kazakhstan—a country considered almost servile in its relationship to Moscow—would speak out against Putin, or worse, keep him waiting.

We saw Putin's choice to invade as irrational and risky, but Putin did not. While this is worth puzzling over, let's first take a step back. Events on the ground as well as an investigation by the *Washington Post*—"Russia's spies misread Ukraine and misled Kremlin as war loomed"—revealed that the Kremlin made gross miscalculations. Russia not only overestimated itself, it also vastly underestimated Ukraine, the willpower of the Ukrainians, and the swift reaction of its allies. Putin misestimated because none of his generals had the courage to tell him that his army was actually smaller than official figures suggested. Basically, his commanders invent phantom troops, pocket the salaries that were supposed to be paid to the non-existent soldiers, and steal entire columns of tanks. His Federal Service of Security (FSB) agents present him with a distorted, sugar-coated version of the kind of welcome his troops will receive in Russian-speaking areas once they cross the border. Maybe they're afraid of the consequences of giving their leader bad news, or maybe they're less infallible than our romanticized image of them would suggest, or perhaps a combination of the two. Whatever the case, Putin's FSB agents actually booked hotel rooms and tables in Kyiv's finest restaurants, confident that it would only take a few days—that the psychological pressure on Zelensky caused by the Russian army entering his country would cause him to crumble—for Russia to take over leadership of the capital of Ukraine.

And then there's the cultural prejudice that permeates the Kremlin's evaluations: Ukrainians were supposed to be a non-people who speak a non-language and have a non-culture, who owe their existence to Russia and Lenin, and who are regularly seen as "our idiotic cousins," incapable of fending for themselves. In a speech given on February 21, 2022, Putin defined Ukraine as "a failed state."

Putin's mistake of overestimating himself and underestimating his victim was no one's fault but his own, but that he also misjudged Kyiv's allies was probably our own doing. In the 2014 invasion, he witnessed the indifference of the European Union—which included two major customers of Russian gas, Germany and Italy. He saw Donald Trump hastily abandon the Kurdish (and Afghan) allies of the United States. He heard Barack Obama say, in 2012, that he was drawing "a red line" in Syria against Putin's own protégé, Bashar al-Assad, and he then saw Obama disrespect the very line he had drawn when Assad used chemical weapons against the rebels. At the time, we naturally all wondered, isn't it a dangerously dramatic sign to draw a red line if you don't intend to respect it? Wouldn't it be better not to draw red lines?

Putin had even heard Joe Biden babble—on live TV—about how helpful the Taliban were proving to be in the fight against terrorism. To this day, the Taliban are on the United States' blacklist of terrorist groups; they were the ones who hosted the training camps for Al Qaeda, the group responsible for the most dramatic terrorist attack in history, the killing of 2977 people at the World Trade Center. The powerful Interior Minister of Afghanistan, Sirajuddin Haqqani, the son of Osama bin Laden's mentor, has a million-dollar bounty on his head for terrorism issued by the American government; in August 2022, he protected the leader of Al Qaeda, Ayman al-Zawahiri, by hosting him in a luxurious apartment in Kabul.

Biden's words were part of a disastrous speech aimed at justifying why the Americans and the entire international coalition withdrew from Kabul on August 15, 2021. Vladimir Putin must have watched them flee with enormous satisfaction. He probably thought that the rest of the world would never have the desire, strength, or patience to help Kyiv—that it was no longer willing to take on arduous and draining commitments beyond its borders.

Two months and a few days after the withdrawal from Afghanistan, close to two hundred thousand Russian troops were in position on the borders of Ukraine. The timing suggests that deployment had been planned for years and that simulations had already been carried out.

Moscow's war of aggression is unique in that there was no real *casus belli* to justify it. (Any comments made about "NATO overreaching" or fake stories about the "genocide in Donbas" were eight-year-old arguments and therefore couldn't be considered provocations in early 2022.) Analysts wonder if it was actually a show of weakness—and not of strength—by freer, more democratic countries that triggered the Russian president's violent, expansionist dreams. To what extent did the failure in Afghanistan lead Putin to think that the propitious moment to move his soldiers had come?

Most Ukrainians stand by the counterfactual hypothesis set out at the beginning of this section, saying, when they broach the topic with a foreigner, "The war started long before you realized it." The implication being: if you had realized it sooner, if you had acted faster, if you had sent different signals to Putin, we would have avoided a conflict of this magnitude, and there would not be this global economic and security crisis. In 2014, the price Putin was forced to pay was small, and Europe failed to reduce its dependence on Russian gas—first to its peril, then its detriment. In 2014, with Russia's occupation of Crimea, Putin reached the absolute peak of consensus in his twenty-year hold on power, and only faced symbolic sanctions as punishment. From the Kremlin's point of view, the idea of invading Ukraine was not at all irrational.

Hatred

To fully understand why Ukrainians don't trust Russia, and why their resentment—from 2014 on—has turned into a form of hatred that will take generations to heal, if at all, we need to believe them when they say, "The war started long before you realized it."

While I was in Kyiv, Kateryna took me to a punk rock concert. Performing that night were Sobaky v Kosmosi (The Dogs of the Cosmos), a band headed by Serhiy Zhadan, a famous Ukrainian writer whose work has been translated into many languages, including English. Serhiy invited me backstage to the green room, where fellow musicians, friends, and girlfriends sat around a table crowded with beer bottles, vodka bottles, and plastic cups. Serhiy comes from Russian-speaking eastern Ukraine but made a political choice to study Ukrainian philology at university and, for a period, taught Ukrainian to middle and elementary school children, but he earns better as a musician. Although Russian was never banned in Ukraine, it was removed from the list of official languages. As a result, identity cards and other documents are written exclusively in Ukrainian, and—in theory—Russian is no longer taught in schools.

The concert begins. Serhiy takes the stage in his leather motorcycle jacket. He has one long lock of blonde hair in the middle of his shaved head. War has been part of his life for the past nine years; many of his fans are fighters and veterans from Donbas. Anton Norokov tells me how Serhiy was locked in a cage in a basement after the separatists took over the city, because he had taken part in Euromaidan marches. He was kept there for weeks and received food every other day. He managed to escape thanks to a sympathetic "enemy," a separatist who had been his classmate at elementary school. Anton was also spared thanks to this same friend.

Another friend in the audience that evening is Sokil. "I wasn't born in Donbas; I went there to fight, and I came back like this." Sokil is a bodybuilder with a prosthetic leg and a bullet fragment lodged at the base of his heart. "The Russian technique is to wound a man but not kill him. The snipers wait for rescuers to come, at which point they have an advantage because the Ukrainians are on a rescue mission, and then they shoot to kill." This happened often in Ukraine prior to February 24, 2022. Every week, the news showed photos of young men who had died in the eastern part of the country.

Sokil was friends with Yaroslav Zhuravel and fought in his squadron. Zhuravel is renowned in Kyiv and throughout Ukraine. Once he managed to get three hundred meters behind the separatists' lines, steal some weapons, and make his way back. His goal was to prove that the rifles used by the separatists were issued by the Russian army. At the time, Moscow's involvement had not yet been proven. Thanks to his stealthy operation, Zhuravel provided the first critical evidence to his government and to the world. This proof was later used by Kyiv to ask the European Commission to apply pressure on Russia with sanctions.

Zhuravel went on to do even more. He infiltrated enemy territory once again and went after something of greater importance: Russian soldiers. He killed six and captured four. He dragged them back to Ukraine alive, showing everyone that the war was not just an internal affair, but that Vladimir Putin was behind it all. Zhuravel's missions were so exceptional that British secret service instructors teach them to new recruits, and they've ended up in MI6 handbooks.

Then came the live television report of Zhuravel's three-day-long death. I heard about it from his father. "Yaroslav was on a scouting mission when a member of his unit was wounded.

They went back to organize a rescue and retrieve him; Yaroslav asked for a temporary ceasefire to carry out the evacuation." A special European Union mission monitored the ceasefires in Donbas. "Dressed in white and wearing a white helmet to signal a rescue operation, Yaroslav and his men went to retrieve the wounded soldier. Despite the ceasefire and the fact that he was wearing white, a Russian sniper shot him. The other soldiers, realizing that the Russians would not respect the ceasefire, fled, leaving Yaroslav on the ground, bleeding but alive." He stayed there, "bleeding but alive," for three days. A Ukrainian military drone filmed him the entire time. He tried to dress his own wounds, to tear off shreds of fabric to stop the bleeding, waving away the drone as if it were a fly.

His father went on. "He must have thought to himself: with all I've done for you—" he stops and corrects himself, "—for us, if you're not going to come and save me, at least stop signaling to the enemy that I'm still alive, and I'll try to save myself." Yaroslav realized that no one would come for him. If reinforcements had been sent in, the Russians would have fired on them. The footage of his agony is now public; millions of Ukrainians have viewed it countless times. In October 2021, at the age of fifteen, Yaroslav's youngest daughter took her oath as a cadet in military high school. She was waiting to come of age so she could "go and fight the same war as her father, and avenge his death," her grandfather told me.

It was from him that I first heard "The war started long before you realized it." On February 24, 2022, the Ukrainians were ready, but we were still in the dark.

When I returned to Ukraine for the fourth time, in September 2022, seven months after the start of the war, the Ukrainian people's hatred had transformed into something far more sophisticated.

I was following the army's progress through the Kharkiv region: the counteroffensive had broken through Russian lines for a distance of ninety kilometers, all the way to Kupyansk, which the Russians had taken almost immediately and where they felt safe. Kupyansk was the city that Russian senator Andrey Turchak visited and proclaimed "Russian forever," saying that the schools had reopened under a Russian curriculum. This came after Ukrainian secondary school textbooks were destroyed and teachers were temporarily deported to the Russian region of Belgorod to learn the new version of history they would have to teach from that moment forward.

On August 29, President Zelensky announced that the counteroffensive had begun. Nobody ever expected them to reach that far, and it was only then that Moscow realized that the Ukrainians were going to attack, and not just in the South, as they had been saying for months.

On August 29, in the village of Nechvolodivka and others in the district of Kupyansk, hundreds of Ukrainian teenagers were put on buses and escorted by Russian military vehicles across the border. After spending the night in Belgorod, they set off again for Gelendzhik, a city by the sea in southern Russia, more than a thousand kilometers from the small houses of Nechvolodivka. "When Ukrainian troops returned, I was filled with an emotion that I can't describe, that I'd never felt before, a combination of both reassurance and alarm," says Ludmila, the mother of thirteen-year-old Veronika, who shares a room with Alexandra in Gelendzhik. "I had hoped the counteroffensive would arrive before my daughter was taken by the Russians, or at least right after she came back. Then I started to wonder if the people in charge knew what they were doing; not even the soldiers know what is going on. Maybe there will be an exchange of prisoners?"

Russian soldiers captured during the counteroffensive in exchange for thirteen-year-olds kidnapped from their homes and villages? Was that the idea?

The mothers in those villages had no internet: the Russians

had succeeded in disconnecting it, and the Ukrainians had not yet restored the service. They had not heard from their children for days. Back at my hotel, I managed to find Alexandra, Veronika's roommate, on Instagram. She replied to me in a chat from Gelendzhik:

—They told us that we start school in two days. It's strange because we were supposed to go back to school on September 1 in Nechvolodivka, but then we had to leave. What's going on? How is everyone at home?

I reassure her.

—There's no water or heat, but everyone is fine. Your grandmother sends you "a world of kisses."

Alexandra is an orphan and lived in Nechvolodivka with her grandmother, Tatyana, who says, "The Russians won't hurt her. She's having a great time. She'll be home in a couple of days."

But Ludmila, Veronika's mother, counters her. "That's not true. You don't know that for sure. We don't have Internet, so you can't have spoken to her."

I speak up. "If you haven't had internet since February 27, how do you hear about the war? Did you hear what happened in Mariupol?"

"No, what happened in Mariupol?"

When Tatyana steps away, Ludmila explains that Alexandra's grandmother will defend the Russians until her granddaughter comes home safely.

"Aren't you afraid they'll use your daughter as a bargaining chip, to ask you for something in return?"

"If we still had Internet, I would have already received a message on Instagram from my daughter asking me to send her the position of the Ukrainian artillery in the forest nearby, so that the Russians could attack them." The Russians use children as their final weapon to maintain some kind of power over the inhabitants of recently liberated villages.

It was around this time that I attended an evening of Ukrainian stand-up comedy. I wondered how the Ukrainians could possibly make people laugh, and about what, with war going on at home. I met four comedians in their late twenties and early thirties. The walls of the basement club were plastered with photos of famous stand-up comedians such as Louis C.K. We talk a little about his sketches: the men love him, while Olga, the only woman comedian present, says, "As a comic he's good, less so as a person." Her husband is fighting in the counteroffensive while she's there to laugh and to make other people laugh: "That's life, full of contradictions. Humans are complex creatures that are forced to sustain thousands of contradictions to live or—in our case—to survive."

Olga had been a contestant on a popular television program, a talent show for comedians, when Zelensky was one of the judges. Around that time, with the Ukrainian counteroffensive having a series of successes, someone created a meme that replaced one of the contestants on the show with a news clip of the Russian Minister of Defense denying the counteroffensive and saying, "Our soldiers in Blaklya, Kupyansk, and Izjum," the cities that had just been liberated, "have merely been repositioned for strategic reasons," followed by a clip of Zelensky in the judge's seat, laughing his head off.

The five stand-up comedians, like almost everyone else their age that I met in Ukraine, had not voted for Zelensky. They had a unique vantage point from which to judge him:

"Before the invasion, I didn't like him as a president, but I liked him even less as a comic."

"As a comedian, Zelensky was not funny. But, as a politician and president, before the war started, he was very funny. Actually, that was probably the only time in his life that he managed to make people laugh."

War never stopped the five comics from performing. Even on February 25, the day after the invasion, when everyone was locked in their homes or bomb shelters, they went on YouTube and started to live stream.

"Sure, we talk a lot about death," one of them tells me. "Leaving death out of our routines would be crazy. It would seem unrealistic to the people who like our humor. And mostly, it wouldn't work for us, up on stage."

"Can you give an example?" I ask. "I mean, it must be hard to talk about these things, given how recent they are . . . "

"Obviously, we don't make fun of the victims. We make fun of the Russians. For us, a dead Russian soldier is a very funny topic. Is that a problem for you?"

"Nothing is a problem for me; I'm here to listen," I reply.

"We hate the Russians." I don't let myself be provoked, but it's the first time they've spoken without a hint of irony, multiple meanings, or nuance. "We have a problem with the Russians. There are endless ways of sugarcoating it, but that's not our job. That's the politicians' job. Our job is to say things as they are. The truth is that Russian soldiers are killing us and that the Russian people are okay with that. Everyone knows it, but only we say it."

I had been eager to meet the comedians because irony has always been a key to the Ukrainian resistance movement. There have been endless memes that play on the sinking of the Russian flagship Moskva ("Russian warship actually fucks itself," "Operation Z; Operation Control Z," "Heroic cruiser Moskva promoted to submarine") and the sabotage of the Kerch bridge that connects the occupied Crimean peninsula to Russia ("Putin's table urgently deployed to Crimea to replace Kerch bridge"). Someone even uploaded images of the burning bridge to the song "Love the Way You Lie" by Eminem and Rihanna, the opening lyrics of which go: "Just gonna stand there and watch me burn? Well, that's alright because I like the way it hurts." I was curious to see how they managed to keep people's spirits up and make people laugh when almost everyone had at least one relative fighting at the front, or a friend who had been killed in the bombings, and instead I discovered a subject that is impossible to avoid in Ukraine today: hatred.

While walking down the streets of recently liberated Kupyansk, I came across three beautiful sixteen-year-old girls filming themselves while tearing down a giant Russian propaganda poster and painting a Ukrainian flag in its place. One of them had long blonde hair and an icy gaze that she seemed to use to conceal her suffering from me, a stranger. "Too bad the Russian soldiers ran away without even putting up a fight," she said. "I would've liked to make sure that my 'new boyfriend,' whom I didn't get to choose, a Russian soldier and an alcoholic, had been killed." She had run after Ukrainian soldiers who were busily doing their jobs to ask them if they'd managed to kill her rapist; she described him with words and gestures, she showed them photos on her phone that she had managed to take of his uniform while he was in the bathroom.

Once, I took part in a debate in Italy, during which a retired political leader argued in favor of a ceasefire that would allow Vladimir Putin to keep the territories that he had thus far occupied. We, she said—and she meant the countries that support Ukraine—needed to tell Kyiv that they should stop their retaliatory actions, that the Ukrainians should stop being so violent. "We need to make sure the Ukrainians behave themselves," this person said. They did not behave. In the days that followed, two Ukrainian citizens stabbed two Russian soldiers while they were walking along the seafront. Ukrainians set off car bombs. They shot through the windows of houses that the Russians had seized.

"We" Europeans or Italians can do many things, but we cannot govern the feelings and reactions of teenagers who have been raped, children whose soldier-parents have been mutilated, men whose pregnant wives died during hospital bombings, parents whose children have been kidnapped and deported to Russia for months at a time, given up for adoption to other local families, or kept indefinitely in Siberian "summer camps." Your suggestion, I later said to the woman in private, is a bit like letting a murderer live in an apartment next to the family of his victim, and telling the family: "Behave." The idea is not just wrong, it's so naive that it is embarrassing for the person who has to respond to it. While a diplomatic roundtable can achieve some things, it will certainly not be able to quell the hatred of the Ukrainians for the Russians. That will take a hundred years, or more.

IV.
Putin's Mistake

The point of no return

Hatred for Putin had been building for years, but it reached a point of no return in March 2022.

Mariupol is a large city by the sea, the size of Miami, with almost half a million inhabitants—half a million Russian-speakers from the Donbas, the population that Putin said he wanted to protect from Kyiv with this war. In less than six weeks since the fighting began, he killed twenty-three thousand people: one in twelve. About a quarter of the city's inhabitants managed to escape immediately, but almost three hundred thousand remained trapped.

"I was standing in the middle of the street, watching the flight path of Russian planes, trying to figure out who or what they were trying to annihilate this time. I was convinced that I'd be safe. After surviving a hundred bombs, you either trick yourself into believing that you're invincible and keep walking, or you freeze and go crazy. That was bomb number 100. Bomb number 101 landed two meters away, in the direction I was running; it landed on my sister and mother." Maria Kutnyakova, a thirty-year-old survivor from Mariupol, told me about her experience for a special report I wrote on Mariupol for the Italian newspaper, *Il Foglio*.

On Christmas Eve 2022, an explosion was heard, followed by a heavy thud and a resounding echo reminiscent of sounds heard the previous spring. But this was not fighting; this was the sound of the Russians demolishing what was left of the Donetsk

Regional Academic Drama Theatre, together with all evidence of their crimes. On March 16, 2022, the Russian word for children, дети, was painted in three-meter-tall letters in front and in back of the Theater, a warning meant to catch the eye of jet fighter pilots—like the one who dropped a bomb on the building. A grey tower of smoke, twice as high as the buildings next to it, rose above the bodies of both the victims and survivors of the most serious Russian attack against Ukrainian civilians in a year of war. At the time, the Theater housed over a thousand civilians, and at least six hundred of them died.[29]

"I was on my way back to the Theater. I had gone out to get some food from my uncle, as my own refrigerator, cupboards, and my entire apartment were gone." Like many other families, Maria had moved into the basement of the Theatre when she was left homeless. "So, I ran towards the flames. People covered in black soot came running out from underground. A Russian sniper shot a wounded woman as she was making her way to the exit. It was as if we were ants and they had set fire to an anthill to make us come out, and then crushed us." Maria had a panic attack that, in hindsight, she considers "a kind of enlightenment," during which she managed to process a lot of information quickly. "I ran away from people. Up until then, I had always followed a different rule: stay away from soldiers, stay away from weapons, stay close to people. I had always tried not to get lost, and to stay with others, either in a hospital or a theatre." But in Mariupol, the rules were different. The Russians did not see people as an obstacle that stood in the way of their target; they were the target. "It occurred to me that if we all run in different directions, they can't kill everyone." Maria saw a crowd of people making the mistake of running for shelter, but she couldn't stop them. "We were all screaming, and no one was listening." Those people ran to a new shelter, the Mariupol Philharmonic, which was demolished by Russian artillery twenty minutes later.

After the bombing of the Theatre, Mariupol became the symbol of Ukrainian resistance; they held the city for eighty-two days, from February 24 to May 20, 2022. But the Russians would not back down—the city was located in the middle of the newly occupied and precious corridor that goes from the Donbas to Crimea—and they showed this by going on the rampage over the rubble for months. When the siege ended, ninety-five percent of the city's buildings were damaged or destroyed. At the end of March, the Russians had the upper hand. For Kyiv, the city was irretrievably lost, but two thousand fighters—mainly Azov soldiers—and more than a thousand civilians (including the families of the soldiers), barricaded themselves inside the tunnels that run for ten thousand square kilometers under the Azovstal steelworks. Thanks to Budanov's mission-impossible-style operations, the head of military intelligence managed to bring supplies to the men and women hiding in the large bunker by flying helicopters low over the occupied territories.

"Enough of this senseless resistance," Moscow said, bothered by the loss of weapons and resources. On April 19, to definitively end the matter, the Russian Ministry of Defense made a proposal: if the Azov fighters surrendered and left the steelworks, unarmed, with the civilians, they would all be spared. The battalion refused the offer even though Volodymyr Zelensky personally asked them to accept it.

To understand this level of obstinacy, which borders on madness, it's necessary to look at the past and go back to the maxim repeated by Ukrainians to foreigners: "The war started long before you realized it." In 2014, soldiers from Kyiv were in a similarly desperate situation in the town of Ilovaisk, another area of the Donbas. On Ukrainian independence day, August 24, they managed to surround the Russian separatists in Ilovaisk, but then found themselves, in turn, surrounded. Vladimir Putin promised the men from Kyiv a safe escape route if they surrendered, and convinced the Ukrainian government to accept the offer. The soldiers obeyed and left Ilovaisk by passing through Moscow's "secure" corridors. While retreating, white flags draped over their military vehicles and thoughts of safety in their heads, they were bombed by pro-Russian forces. Three hundred sixty-six people died. This was the bloodiest massacre for Kyiv in the entire Donbas war prior to the 2022 invasion. At the time, survivors and relatives of soldiers who were killed largely blamed their own government for having acted naively, for sending their men in to be massacred, and for giving up the city to the enemy.

Ilovaisk is one of the reasons the Azovstal resistance lasted longer than Zelensky himself would have liked, and why Ukrainians refuse to accept hypothetical compromises that might seem reasonable or advantageous to us on the outside. After years of deception and traps, many Ukrainians believe that, in an agreement with Putin, the Russian leader will end up taking not only what the pact guarantees him legally but also, by force, what he had promised to give up or spare. Putin needs to be physically forced out; only material limits work with him, not legal ones.

The Russian conquest of Crimea is another event that Ukrainians say foreigners do not fully understand. Not only is it an illegally occupied peninsula, it is a strategic territory and an indispensable launching pad used by Moscow to acquire other parts of the country in 2022, and Mariupol above all. In a period of ten months after the full-scale invasion, eight hundred attacks against Ukrainian cities were launched from Crimea, which the Russians have transformed into one giant military base. If Putin had not occupied Crimea in 2014, he would not have managed to conquer close to twenty percent of Ukraine eight years later.

In April 2022, I meet Katya, a 31-year-old volunteer who was born and lives in Mariupol. In the past two months, she has grown very thin; she no longer resembles her profile picture on WhatsApp, nor does she look her age. She has just fled from Mariupol against her will. "I shouldn't be here. Now, more than ever, Mariupol needs me." But she had to follow orders from the leaders of the volunteer group of which she is part. The Russians are no longer at the borders, they have entered the city, the soldiers are fighting in the streets, and Kyiv fears retaliation against the volunteers whom Russian propaganda calls neo-Nazis from Pravy Sektor, or the "Right Sector," a far-right and ultranationalist political organization.

I ask Katya about a commonly heard accusation: that the Azov battalion, now part of the Ukrainian army, used civilians from Mariupol as human shields, effectively trapping them in the surrounded city and preventing them from escaping. "I could have left whenever I wanted, I just didn't want to. But at a certain point, I was forced to leave. I couldn't stay. Naturally, there were times when the Ukrainian authorities advised us not to use the humanitarian corridors, but that was because they considered them dangerous, they said." Katya believes that the fact that she managed to flee in safety proves her point. Along the route, she went through many Russian checkpoints, with soldiers searching her at least ten times, looking at her phone, and examining her for tattoos. They were particularly interested to see if she had a trident tattoo, the official symbol of Ukraine that many nationalists have gotten inked on their forearms, or a red and black mosaic that is popular among members of far-right militias.

It would be wrong to use the word "peaceful" to describe life in Mariupol today. Russian reconstruction has been only partial, and the residents who fled now call their home "Potemkin city," from the term "Potemkin façade," where a brightly painted cardboard exterior covers a rotted-out building. Katya survived the same bombing that Maria did, the one that hit the Theatre. Since that day, her eight-year-old daughter has spoken with a stutter. Her grandparents are still in Mariupol. “People have to queue for hours for bread and rice in minus six degrees Celsius,” Katya tells me. Images taken from above show long lines of people wrapping around buildings, cutting through alleys, and then continuing onto a multi-lane highway. “But the scariest thing is that you can’t trust anyone. You don’t know who you’re talking to, you don’t know the Russians who moved into the apartment next door, which used to belong to your neighbors, who were killed.”

A number of victims have become terrifying individuals. “Some of the traumatized have gone clinically insane and are now dangerous. Drunken men wield knives to get whatever they want: money, sex, food.” While rape has become a constant emergency, looting has become more sophisticated: the Russians have entered branches of abandoned Ukrainian banks in Mariupol, cleared away rubble and detritus, obtained folders and hard drives, and have effectively stolen the data of Ukrainian account holders. By the time the SBU intelligence agency became aware of this, in mid-February 2023, Russians had already entered the data into online interfaces of the bank branches, accessed the accounts, and transferred more than one hundred million hryvnias (over two and a half million euros), belonging to residents of Mariupol, into their own accounts.

Vladimir Putin doesn’t like having to pay for his ungrateful victims’ needs with his own money. The stolen funds were converted into cryptocurrency by pseudo-officials of the government of the self-proclaimed separatist People’s Republic of Donetsk, together with a group of criminals, by using online and telephone banking systems. Thousands of families in Mariupol lost their savings; the Russians have stolen from the living as well as from the dead, “and from people like my parents, who still believe that things can improve, that there will be a future,” Katya tells me.

The private clinics and eight hospital complexes in Mariupol do not have enough beds to treat the city's inhabitants because they're crowded with mutilated Russian soldiers returning from the Donbas front. Hospital 3, a pediatric medical center with a large maternity ward, was bombed by the Russians in March 2022. The most important medical institution, Hospital 2, has five hundred fifty beds; before the war, it had the best intensive care unit in the Donbas region. It is also the only hospital that has drugs for neurological diseases and is the best equipped to treat cancer patients. There have been numerous frenzied attempted robberies of the medical supply warehouses, with the thieves being the ill patients themselves. The more than 100,000 inhabitants who remain in the city live like ghosts, listening to Moscow television broadcast fantastic tales of the "New Mariupol." Road and resurfacing works, which are part of a plan to turn the city into a sparkling "international tourist destination," are continually interrupted by the discovery of corpses, as the populace was forced to bury their neighbors in a hurry, to prevent the spread of disease. For the Russians the "wooly mammoths"—as they call the large steel industries, such as Azovstal in Illich, adopting the local term—are things of the past.

In some kindergartens, cafeterias have been forced to close down because the People's Republic has run out of money. Teachers and principals—either Russian or Ukranian "collaborators"—ask parents to pay them two hundred rubles under the counter to feed their children a sandwich when lunchtime rolls around and the kids start to get hungry. "Who has two hundred rubles to spend a day?" Katya wonders. Yet another example of how the Kremlin prefers not to spend its own money to assist the victims of its war.

The counteroffensive and the word "victory" are not just rhetoric to Kyiv. They are shorthand for a concrete project: to bring back food to the cafeterias in Mariupol, restore history books to the shelves, to return beds to the maternity wards for mothers-to-be, to treat infections, identify the dead, and prosecute crimes.

The counteroffensive falls to Commander Nazarii Kishak of the 72nd motorized brigade. Kishak is not an optimist; unlike some of his colleagues, he doesn't use glowing words to describe his battalion. And yet, his battalion is famous in Ukraine for never having retreated from any front. For nine years, Kishak has done nothing but fight the Russians, after already defending Mariupol in 2014. The optimist in his unit is a twenty-eight-year-old whose nom de guerre is Marik, from Mars, the god of war. Marik is from Mariupol, which he calls "the shining city." He still has friends and family there. "How could I not be optimistic?" Marik asks. He has no doubt that, as soon as conditions allow, the 72nd will descend on Mariupol and he'll be able to go get his motorcycle. He looks forward to riding over to a friend's house for a couple of beers, or going to visit his aunt, and bringing her flowers.

Because Mariupol is just out of range of the American HIMARS rocket launchers, which can reach up to seventy thousand meters, Moscow has turned the city into one large military fortress. The HIMARS allowed Kyiv to succeed in their counteroffensives in Kharkiv and Kherson, avoiding a bloodbath by pre-emptively disarming their enemy with targeted bombings on storage depots. The first time around, when the Russians were left without enough weapons and supplies to continue their fighting, they fled Kharkiv in chaos. The second time, in Kherson, they retreated in an orderly fashion.

The doors of Pryazovskyi University in Mariupol are closed, its library's history books lie in piles on the sidewalk where the main entrance used to be. The windows on the ground floor have been bombed out; the Russians simply toss the books out onto the street through the gaping holes in the walls. They're destined for pulping, part of a broader plan. The Ukrainian

National Library—one of the largest in the world—and its network of more than three hundred regional and university libraries, as well as thousands of school libraries, were destroyed in a single year of battle, too many to be considered "collateral" damage, Oksana Bruy, the president of the Ukrainian Library Association, points out.

Before the Russians begin reconstruction in occupied cities, everything that refers to the very existence of Ukraine—which, for Vladimir Putin, is merely a chimera—is systematically destroyed. As well as everything that refers to Moscow's past crimes. In fact, at the beginning of the invasion, one of Russia's first strikes was a targeted bombing of an archive in the city of Chernihiv that was known for holding the documents regarding the KGB's repression of Ukrainian dissidents and papers concerning the Holodomor, Stalin's genocide of Ukrainian peasants.

Maria managed to escape from Mariupol after the bombing of the Theatre and now lives in Vilnius, Lithuania. "There's no sea here," she says. "I hope that Mariupol is liberated by summer because it drives me crazy to think of Russian soldiers enjoying my beaches. I can't tell you when this war will end, but I know that Mariupol will one day be Ukrainian. I've learnt that history is written by the conquerors; the history of my city simply cannot be written by Putin."

Over time, I've met many eastern Ukrainians who either passively or unhappily accepted the turn of events brought about by Euromaidan. Men like Yura, whose son fights in the Ukrainian army while his ex-wife and teenage daughter live in Moscow—men indifferent to the outcome of the war but with a great deal to lose either way. Or women like Natasha, who furiously smoked her ultra-thin Vogue cigarettes, inhaling continuously, never taking the time to exhale, on the deserted streets of Lyman, under fire from both Russian and Ukrainian artillery. She and her mother have been living in Kyiv-controlled

Donbas since 2014, while her sister is with the separatists in Donetsk. People like Natasha never felt the urgent need to free Ukraine from Moscow's control, and for a long time, they were closely tied to the world of Russia and even to Putin. But all that changed after the siege of Mariupol. The massacre in Donbas of Russian-speaking civilians like themselves changed their perception of Putin. Even though the president said he wanted to protect the people of Donbas, he ended up punishing them more harshly than the rest of the Ukrainians, whom he explicitly considered his enemies. Everything that Maria Kutnyakova told me about the history books and her deep desire to return to the beaches of Mariupol corresponds to the sentiment of a nation that saw that city as the symbol of unforgettable and absolute violence, driving its people to react with resolve instead of fear.

A Russian refutes Russia

At the beginning of the war, Putin didn't dare carpet bomb Kyiv because he didn't want to jeopardize the possibility, which he initially considered feasible, that Ukraine—which is to say Zelensky—would surrender. Doing to Kyiv what was done to Grozny in Chechnya, or to Aleppo in Syria, or to Mariupol would have made it impossible for Putin to govern the Ukrainians after a surrender. And it would've been counterproductive in case the capital were soon to fall into his hands. The Russians had no strategy in place for how they might govern the Ukrainians, but at the beginning of the war, this wasn't clear to anyone—not in Moscow, Brussels, or Washington.

Putin ruthlessly bombed the Russian-speaking people of the east in the same way that he bombed Chernihiv, a city in the north positioned along one of the invasion routes from Belarus. On April 1, 2022, I tried to enter Chernihiv, which had been isolated from the rest of the world for a month, surrounded by Russians and bombed from the sky. The population of the city at the time was just shy of 100,000, but up until two months earlier, it had three times as many inhabitants. At the end of March, when the Kremlin realized that it wouldn't be able to conquer the regional capital and that it was wasting ammunition, tanks, and soldiers there, it started to withdraw from northwestern Ukraine. When I arrived, the Russians were still leaving the area. No journalists, neither Ukrainian nor foreign, had yet set foot in the city.

Danger was everywhere. It was like walking a tightrope. While leaving, the Russians blew up bridges and placed landmines on the roads and fields. It was practically impossible to know with any accuracy, in real time, if a particular area of woodland was still occupied or not. Even though we were thirty kilometers away from Moscow's military vehicles, we were still within range of their artillery: all they had to do was turn their cannons around. The highway I traveled with a volunteer, Vitalyk, and his girlfriend was pitted with craters, lined with exploded tanks, animal carcasses, and tree trunks. Twice we got a flat tire. Two days earlier, another group of volunteers and a Ukrainian parliamentarian had travelled the same route; their van was still there, a burnt-out shell. One of the volunteers and the parliamentarian were killed. Several Spanish journalists were injured by shrapnel.

There has been no press coverage from within the city for a month. People on the outside knew little or nothing about the people who were trapped inside. But that wasn't the only reason I traveled there; I had a more specific mission. Nikita, a young friend who lives in Latina, Italy, but was born in Chernihiv, told me that neither he nor his mother, Valentina, has had news of his great-grandfather, Vladimir, for a month. Vladimir turned 96 on March 8, 2022. No one knew if he was alive or dead, if his house had been bombed or not. Although the phone lines had been restored, he had not answered his phone.

The following day, April 2, I make my way down the city

streets with Google Maps open on my phone, searching for the red apartment building where Vladimir lives. A few people are out in the streets, most of them are drunk. Electricity is back and—in some places—there's even internet. There's still no heat (last night the temperature was negative eight degrees Celsius) and no running water. Tents rigged to wooden electricity poles along the road have functioned as toilets for the inhabitants of Chernihiv for the past month. Near the main square, a man in uniform shoots out light bulbs in a semi-demolished building; when the electricity came back, the lights turned on automatically, and in an effort not to overload the fragile grid, lights such as these need to be turned off. Shooting them out is the only way.

Over the past month, the Russians aimed their bombs at the center of town, railway lines, construction sites, a psychiatric hospital, survivors lining up for bread, and the oncology department of a clinic. I slept in the basement of Hospital 4 until the Russians began their retreat and the Ukrainians started to come out of the shelters. There had been one hundred eighty of us, with families forced to share one full-size mattress.

After the Russians retreated from Chernihiv and we discovered the extent of their massacres, people had to decide if they should start living again, or if it was too soon. Refugees in the hospital even slept in the archives, on mattresses they squeezed between the filing cabinets. When the city was under siege, three ill patients who could effectively survive on their own were discharged and went home. Of the thirty-six who remained, twenty-two died—and not from the bombs, but from cold, lack of hygiene, and the absence of medical care.

Olha lived in the hospital shelter with her boyfriend the entire time; her home had no basement, and she had nowhere else to go. She was twenty-seven and very tall. Over the course of that month, she could only brush her teeth twice a week: they had to save water, which they needed to share. Washing was not a priority; boiling the water, cooling it, and drinking it was. Once the Russians left, after two days without bombs, and with the return of electricity but still no water, Olha left the shelter, went up to the third floor, and retrieved her large duffel bag and hair straightener. "To escape, you need money. I'm not rich enough. I have to wait and see if the owner of the shop where I work decides to reopen."

The people of Chernihiv overcame their fear of death, but dealing with the aftermath is difficult. Rebuilding and starting over is costly, both in terms of money and effort—and then there's the question of trust. "We want to believe that it's all over, that the Russians have left for good, but no one's really sure of that." Even so, young people move concrete blocks away from the bombed-out buildings and the destroyed power station. Women sweep broken glass and rubble off the asphalt. Once the bombing stopped, the instinct is to clean up.

I make my way to the spot indicated on Google Maps. I see a reddish building, but it's not accessible from the road. I call Nikita for instructions, and he passes me his mother, Valentina. Her anxious voice guides me forward.

"You need to enter from the back. Go around the building."

I do as I'm told. The door is locked shut.

"I don't recall it ever being closed. They're probably afraid. Thieves go in bombed-out buildings to steal things that the residents were forced to leave behind."

Two ladies walk by, dragging plastic shopping carts full of broken glass.

"Put them on the phone. They know him for sure."

With Valentina on speaker phone, they accompany me to a green metal side door that leads to the wing of the building where Vladimir's apartment, number 50, is located. The entrance is locked. A man looks down from the first-floor balcony; after a month of living under siege with no communication, people's initial reaction is distrust. They expect looters and

Russian spies, the authorities told them not to open or talk to anyone, but to wait for the SBU agents. I say nothing but stand on tiptoe and hold the phone up as high as I can. Valentina's pleas in Ukrainian convince him. He comes down, opens the door for me, and, without saying a word, accompanies me to apartment number 50. I press the buzzer for five full seconds and then wait. A lady with a scarf wrapped around her head and wearing three sweaters opens the door. I look behind her: I catch a glimpse of a long-haired ginger cat, then a second cat, and finally an elderly man.

"He's here!" I cry out. Valentina begins talking rapidly and crying at the same time.

"Put the lady on the phone so I can talk to her! That's Anna Ivanovna. She's a friend of ours!"

Valentina pummels Anna with questions, and she replies with a smile. Vladimir understands and tries to speak on the phone in his weak voice. "I'm alive! I'm alive!" he says.

Vladimir survived the month-long bombing in his freezing cold apartment. Too old to make his way down into the cellar with everyone else, he sat in his armchair, as far away from the windows as possible, on the third floor, just listening to the explosions. Every day, someone brought him food and drink, but he had to stay there, exposed to missiles and bombs.

After they talk for a bit, the cell phone ends up back in my hands. Valentina tells me to look around his home, to ask him about the memorabilia and the photos. "Get him to tell you everything. My grandfather is a war hero. Get him to show you his medals."

Vladimir asks me if I know how many people were killed. I tell him that, for now, there have been three hundred civilian deaths, but the number will surely increase. The Russians were busy bombing Chernihiv up until a few hours ago, and only recently have people started to dig under the rubble, looking for victims.

"And soldiers? How many young men were killed?"

"We don't know how many Ukrainian soldiers have been killed; it's a military secret."

"Fine. What about the Russians? How many young Russian soldiers died?"

I tell him that Kyiv reports that eighteen thousand soldiers were killed, but Moscow says fewer than two thousand.

Vladimir is Russian. He never applied for Ukrainian citizenship. He shows me his Russian passport. He was a colonel in the Red Army. He considers the Russian soldiers to be part of a large family, with him one of its oldest members. "In the past, a person was proud to be part of that family. Today, it is painful to belong to it."

A wooden bookcase holds a wrought-iron hammer and sickle from the 1970s, and a display cabinet shows portraits of generals and photos of him in a Red Army infantry hat, surrounded by children and grandchildren. In one photo, he's even holding Nikita as an infant.

Vladimir was not forced to go to war. It was a choice that he made, he had to insist on it and even deceive the authorities of the Soviet Union, "for the greater good." Vladimir was not yet eighteen when he enrolled, and he had to forge his documents. He wouldn't have been allowed to go to the front, both because of his young age and because a law required him to stay at home and care for his mother. "A person's reason for going to war is everything." In this war, thousands of young Russian men ended up at the front in a disorderly manner, believing they were just taking part in a simulation, only realizing they were at war with Ukraine when they crossed the border on February 24, 2022. "We, on the other hand, wanted to defend ourselves from Adolf Hitler. Being in a trench is horrifying: you're afraid of dying, and you're surrounded by corpses that look just like you. It's impossible to endure if you don't know why you're there, if you don't have a clear motivation."

Vladimir fought "the real Nazis" in Ukraine eighty years ago. Now in his nineties, he is being bombed by his Russian fellow citizens in what—I tell him—Vladimir Putin calls "an operation of denazification."

"My life is a paradox. Putin's war is a paradox," he says as he overturns a drawerful of medals and small, shiny insignia onto the sofa, handed to him by Anna.

"They destroyed my city and killed my neighbors in order to 'denazify' the country? No, and I am living proof of it. This is a genocide of Ukrainians and young Russians, and a nightmare for their mothers, who will never be able to make sense of their grief."

For Vladimir, it's a twofold tragedy, a blatant short-circuit. "Aren't they aware of the absurdity of it all? Doesn't the Kremlin know that we are all Slavs, that millions of Ukrainians live in Russia, and vice versa? That there are soldiers here in Chernihiv who have sisters who study at the University of Moscow? They need to show a little respect for our history! Ours was a grand history."

Tricking Putin

In this, Vladimir Putin was not very careful about his propaganda and choice of words. The rhetoric endorsed by the Russian government was irregular, inconsistent, paradoxical, and full of afterthoughts. The term "denazification," which surprised and offended retired Red Army colonel Vladimir, was ineffective and dropped a few months after it was trotted out, even by those who had initially believed the concept. Ukrainians who spent time with Russians during periods of occupation told me how frustrated the Russian soldiers were not to find tattoos with runes, swastikas on the walls, or busts of Hitler—things that had been promised them, and which would have alleviated the hard work of killing.

The use of "denazification" was intended to evoke a war

that the Russians are obviously proud of, one that they continue to commemorate each year with the Victory Parade, a war in which Vladimir himself participated. And yet, the questionable comparison didn't even catch on with an audience generally inclined to accept whatever Putin says. As a result, the Kremlin quickly stopped using the term in public speeches, and the rhetoric was altered so that the war was not presented as another war against Nazism, but a war that was needed to protect Russia's children from the West, who wanted to "undermine and divide" Russian society.

In terms of international communications, a topic generally of interest to Putin, presenting the invasion as an "operation to denazify Ukraine" was a hasty choice. The president of the country being invaded, and therefore theoretically the leader of the Nazis, actually has Jewish origins, and—despite being criticized for being too soft on Putin—has often clashed with Ukrainian far-right militias. As a matter of fact, in 2019, Azov and the Right Sector started their own campaign against Zelensky's strategy to bring peace to Donbas: they opposed the Minsk agreements, violated them the same way the separatists did, and started a rebel movement against Kyiv's participation in the pact and against the president by endorsing a policy they called "No to capitulation." Andriy Biletsky, the commander of the Azov battalion and leader of the far-right party, National Corps (which won two percent in the 2019 elections), threatened Zelensky in a none-too-veiled manner and raged against the president in furious tones.

Zelensky went to the trenches in Donbas to make peace with those men, to say, "set down your arms; it's not me you should be fighting." But it didn't work. What ought to have been a truce turned into an argument in front of the cameras.[30] Macabre jokes circulated on social media and in the Ukrainian press, suggesting that if Zelensky went back to the front line in Donbas to see the men in those militias, he was risking his life.

"Who knows, he might get blown to pieces by a grenade," a Ukrainian parliamentarian from the opposition is reported to have said.

The president made peace with Azov and the Right Sector—at least temporarily—in December 2021, when Russian tanks and soldiers positioned themselves at the border of the country, two months before Russian launched its all-out assault.

Not only was Zelensky never credible as a possible Nazi leader, during an early bombing of Kyiv—at a moment when Putin was supposed to be "denazifying" the country—Russian missiles struck one of the most important Holocaust memorials in the world. The Babi Yar memorial was erected to commemorate the Nazi massacre of September 1941, when more than thirty-three thousand Jews were killed in the ravines outside Kyiv in the first two days alone. In time, the number of victims rose to more than a hundred thousand, the worst massacre of Jews in Ukraine during the Second World War. While Babi Yar was not Putin's target—his goal was to strike the state-owned television tower and eventually managed to do so—the mistake ended up on the front pages of the international press, reminding the whole world that Ukrainians erect monuments to condemn Hitler's crimes, and that Putin's bombs destroy them.

The Russian president has not always been so inept at constructing an alternative vision of reality, later promoted on a global scale. In the past, and recently in Syria, he has skillfully convinced millions of people in Europe and the United States alone—not to mention the rest of the world—of his version of events. Non-Western public opinion—which is to say, the majority of the world—is actually irrelevant to Putin. He is only interested in the kind of public opinion that can democratically influence its governments, which is to say governments willing to help Kyiv. Chinese or Sudanese public opinion is of no interest to him, because no one ever expected Beijing or Khartoum to support the resistance fighters in Kyiv. Which also means that the governments Putin needed to weaken were elsewhere.

Putin is keen on influencing and confusing those who might get in his way, not those who consider the Ukrainian question remote and of little importance. For example, the way the Russian president managed to convince many Westerners that the American bombings in the Middle East were a monstrous show of imperialism, while his bombings in Syria were acts of heroism against terrorism—for which we should all, and Europeans, in particular, who experienced the Islamic State attacks in Paris and Barcelona, thank him—was a masterpiece of global communication. If he didn't fare so well in Ukraine, it is thanks to a woman who is at least as clever as he is, if not more so.

Avril Haines is fifty years old; she has brown hair and a slim, muscular build. Born in Manhattan into a family of scientists, her mother was a painter and died when Avril was fifteen. Haines did well at school but preferred hands-on activities to studying. She worked as a mechanic in a New York auto shop, practiced judo at a high level (like Putin), and studied to become a pilot, eventually marrying her flight instructor. She got a degree in physics, then studied law, but interrupted her studies to take on a very special business initiative. She bought a taproom at auction that had been seized in a drug raid and turned it into an independent bookshop where she organized readings of erotic literature. She named the bookshop after her mother and, convinced of erotica's benefits for relationships, offered half-price discounts to couples.

She then went back to university to get an advanced degree in international law and was later asked to interview for a job with the State Department, which she clinched. Barack Obama eventually chose her for the role of deputy director of the CIA, the first woman to hold this position. When Vladimir Putin started to mobilize his army in preparation for an invasion,

Haines had just broken another record: the first woman in history to head the most important secret service agency in the world. Starting on January 21, 2021, the day after Joe Biden took office at the White House, Haines was placed in charge of coordinating all seventeen American intelligence agencies, responsible for compiling the briefings on world events that the American president read over breakfast.

In the months leading up to a potential war on Europe's doorstep, Haines advised Biden to adopt a new communication strategy and talk openly about everything that was going on.

The goal was to get ahead of Putin, and the basic principle is simple: revealing the enemy's possible moves makes them feel trapped, and can force them to change their plans, if possible. The enemy will feel exposed and under pressure, which allows you to set the tone and direction of the narrative. The objective was to put Putin on the back foot.

In the early months of 2022, the Biden administration shared all kinds of details regarding the movements of Russian forces at the Ukrainian border. With exact precision, Washington communicated when enough soldiers had been gathered at the border to begin a full-scale invasion. The United States also revealed the content of intercepted communications between Russian generals, divulging messages exchanged between the highest members in the chain of command. Washington even mentioned the distinct possibility of Kyiv capitulating in forty-eight hours, scaring the rest of us with the possibility of fifty thousand civilian deaths. In any other war, this kind of information would have remained classified and encrypted, but now the plan was different: sharing everything in real time.

Haines disclosed an intricate Russian plan to create a bogus video that showed Ukrainian soldiers using illegal weapons against the Donbas separatists. By announcing on live television how Moscow would try and spread disinformation, she effectively exposed their plan. The phony video appeared online a few days later anyway—with two fake Ukrainian soldiers holding cylindrical containers described in the captions as canisters of chlorine, a chemical weapon that kills by attacking the airways, leading to suffocation—but it got very few views, and hardly anyone believed it was real.

Putin is a master at information warfare and creating smoke screens. For years, he has shown the world how news, whether true or false, can be used to destabilize an adversary or its allies. Avril Haines may not have stopped the war, but she managed to expose Putin and trick him by revealing his own weapons, turning his art against him. Russia's failure at manipulating communications about the war is no less important than its military failures on the ground, and consequently had a major impact.

According to *The New York Times*, not since the 1960s—during the Cuban Missile Crisis—has American intelligence released so much information or exerted such powerful influence on the media narrative.[31] Putin is no longer a solo player of information warfare; sitting across from him is a woman who ruined his opening move. If Haines had not exposed Putin's plans months in advance, it's likely that many more people in the West would have believed the version that the Russian president wanted us to: we're not attacking, we're responding to an attack that the Ukrainians started. As he has effectively done in the past, Putin sought to reverse the roles of victim and attacker.

And let's not forget that the perception that the general public of Europe and North America has of the war also has a terribly direct impact on the battlefield.

Beyond the front line

Niko stands directly below a skyscraper that has just been hit by a Russian missile. He is on the phone with his mother, who does not believe him. "You're lying!" she says. "There's no war there!"

After getting divorced, Niko's mother moved to Russia and

was remarried to a soldier in the Red Army. I was with Niko when the bombs hit the television tower and the Babi Yar monument, killing four civilians who were driving by, including two children. Niko is twenty-three, he listens to rap music that came out before he was born, and he worked in the film industry as a producer until it was no longer possible to make movies in Ukraine.

His mother frequently asks him why he continues to believe American propaganda. Her version of the facts, which reflects that of her husband and the Kremlin, is that Putin did not start a long-term war but implemented a swift operation of surgical strikes that are so circumscribed, they're invisible to civilian eyes. She's so convinced of this version that she doesn't question it, despite having a witness on the ground whom she generally trusts. The first time Niko tried telling her that some parts of the city of Kyiv, where he lives, explode into flames every day, it did not go over well. She replied by saying that the dead people in Mariupol are all actors and influencers who use fake blood, the kind you can buy in magic shops. Whenever possible, Niko calls her from a devastated area—standing in front of a crumbling skyscraper, a ruined gymnasium, or a burnt-out car—and describes exactly what he sees in front of him, in detail, as if trying to cure her. "But no matter how hard I try, my mother always ends the call by asking me when I'm going to come visit. She's so brainwashed that she actually believes a Ukrainian citizen can travel freely to Russia."

At the time, I was trying to contact a young man in Moscow named Kamran Manafly. I had read one of his opinion pieces on the independent Russian website, Meduza, and I had written to him on Instagram; he only replied after the episode of my podcast, *Stories*, about him was broadcast.

Kamran is twenty-eight and teaches geography at High School 498 in the Tagansky district. "The level of education that Russians generally receive at school is quite high, the textbooks that my colleagues and I use are top-notch. The freedom to teach whatever we want is not questioned: no one knows what we teach, and no one checks what gets said in a Moscow classroom. Everything was going fine, it was all working out well, until the last elections, in September 2021." The teachers who worked at the polling stations counting ballots were "advised" to fudge the numbers. "Our superiors suggested we vote for Putin's party, United Russia. Something like that had never happened before, no one had ever dared."

Up until then, the classroom had been a protected space where a teacher could dialogue with the students in an open manner. "But after February 24, 2022, everything changed." The government sent precise guidelines to each school on how to explain the "special operation" to the students. Teachers receive pre-packaged videos by mail to show during class hours, which include footage of members of the Zelensky government and a voiceover saying that these are members of a Nazi group. Other videos focus on the war crimes committed by Ukrainian militias against pro-Russian separatists. Some are true—such as the 2014 Odessa massacre—while others are invented.

"Do your students believe the propaganda?"

"Some do, but not everyone."

Students gather around Kamran, both in the classroom and in the halls, to ask him about the war. "I answer honestly. I try to relate the facts to them as impartially as possible, so they can make up their own minds. They're capable of judging for themselves." A few days later, the principal calls for a faculty meeting and reprimands some of them, reminding everyone to follow the rules and show the clips in class. At the end of the meeting, the principal says, "As civil servants, you are not allowed to have personal opinions."

These words shook Kamran to the core. They also represented an epiphany to him. "I never thought it would come to that. Things had never been that way. But in that moment, I understood what we were about to become, and how Russia was quickly heading towards a cliff." He takes part in an anti-war demonstration and posts a photo of himself in the main square on Instagram, with the following caption:

> You have to live in such a way that your conscience doesn't torment you. Recently, at school, I was told: "You cannot have any opinion other than the official one, promoted by the State." Well, I have my own opinions! And I am not alone. Many teachers have their own opinions. And you know what? Our opinions don't always align with those of the State. I don't want to just be a mirror of government propaganda, and I'm proud that I'm no longer afraid to write it here. I'm proud to be a teacher. My conscience is clear.
>
> I love every single student I've ever had, have now, and will have.

The principal threatens to fire him for his comment, but Kamran refuses to delete the Instagram post. The following day, the police are waiting for him at the school entrance. He is not allowed to go to his classroom to teach, or even to talk to his students, "not even to say goodbye." The other teachers look on without saying a word. "I knew I was right, and that I wasn't alone." The first thing Kamran does after being turned away from the high school is go to his union office to file an appeal against the school administration. "Suddenly, the people who had always been willing to defend us were no longer able to help. The atmosphere had changed. I'd never seen the union reps in such a bad mood." He realizes that he will be arrested for espionage, so he goes back to his apartment, packs his things, and runs away.

Kamran was not alone. Tens of thousands of young professionals, often those with the best educations and specialized skills, left Russia around the same time. Overall, their departure created greater damage to the Russian economy than the price ceiling imposed on gas. According to Maksut Shadayev, the Russian Minister for Digital Development, one hundred thousand tech specialists left the country since the invasion of Ukraine. But other sources indicate that in the first eleven months of war alone, five hundred thousand Russians relocated to Finland, Turkey, the former Soviet Republics (especially Georgia, Armenia, Kyrgyzstan, and Kazakhstan), and, for those who could afford it, Dubai. A wave of departures continued to erode the Russian population month after month; three hundred thousand men, one percent of all males between the ages of twenty and fifty-five, were called to duty in September 2022.

Minorities, and in particular the Muslim community (which numbers fourteen million people), who were generally considered an inexhaustible and reliable reservoir for the army—and who, up until a few years ago, paid bribes to secure permanent positions in the armed forces—rebelled against this mobilization with unusual violence. While the Orthodox Christian Patriarch Kirill continues to say that the battle in Ukraine is a holy war and that those who fight in it will surely go to heaven, the imams of the country's mosques preached that their followers should refuse to participate in an unjust war.

One year after the start of the war, there were twenty-five thousand fewer births in the Russian Federation; men were either separated from their partners when they were sent to the front, or they fled to avoid being sent to fight. The birth rate decreased to 1.3 children per woman, the absolute lowest in Russian history. In early 2023, Russia also experienced the lowest unemployment rate in its history, at 3.7 %, but this only because so many men had left the country, which made it easy for those who stayed to find work.

Bones in a backpack

At the beginning of the aggression against Ukraine, Russian soldiers were the first to fall prey to Putin's propaganda about "the denazification of Ukraine" and his glorification of the heroes of the Red Army, which led them to compare themselves and their mission to an entirely different kind of war.

Young officers discovered that they were being sent into battle only a few hours before the invasion started, and were only able to inform their subordinates once they had already crossed the border—by which point the soldiers had figured it out themselves. In the early hours of February 24, 2022, lieutenants realized that they didn't have the trust of their commanders, and the commanders didn't have the trust of the armies. At dawn on that first day, the soldiers either believed or convinced themselves they were acting as liberators, but as soon as families in Ukraine woke up and discovered they were at war, they directed their rage, epithets, and ripe tomatoes at the young men riding on armored cars. As the notion of a lightning operation faded, the front lines ran out of fuel and, then, of food, with replenishments never arriving: the soldiers in their heavy tanks were like birds in cages, exposed on all sides to anti-tank missiles.

The Russian apparatus had major logistical problems—miscalculating timing, among other things—and was ultimately responsible for more Russian deaths in the first few weeks than actual fighting, making things far too easy for Ukrainian ambush teams. Those soldiers who managed to reach and occupy villages and towns found themselves living among a rebellious population that they soon came to fear—and with good reason. A hostile local person could easily sell your geographical position to Kyiv and have you killed. The Russian soldiers became more nervous with each passing day and consequently crueler.

Nykola Rudenko is from Ruska Lozova, a village seven kilometers north of Kharkiv, where he lived under occupation until April 29, 2022, when the Ukrainian army liberated the town. The following day, he was able to escape with his wife Julija. "Let's just say I stole a car from a Russian soldier who had stolen it from me three weeks earlier." They made it to the southern border of the village with two Ukrainian tanks flanking them, driving in reverse, while shooting at the enemy.

Nykola told me that the Russian attitude towards their victims transformed quickly. "In war, time is compressed, and their behavior changed suddenly. Initially, they thought we would welcome them, so they treated us pretty well; they weren't rough. On the second day, a couple of them even helped me carry a heavy container of water into my house. But as soon as they noticed someone acting suspicious, or if people suddenly went silent around them, they stiffened up."

As the days passed, and the Russians saw more and more of their comrades die, they started to grow paranoid. "Once a Russian soldier started asking me, 'Where are the eyes of the American devil?' I didn't understand what he meant. He repeated it three times and then started screaming at me. The fourth time he asked, he pointed his Kalashnikov at me," Nykola says, pretending to grip an assault rifle. "They grew obsessed with the Americans, they kept mentioning the CIA, using strange codenames, looking everywhere for proof of them, thinking they'd find them." On April 20, the Russian soldier who had pointed his weapon in Nykola's face aimed it at the cell towers and started shooting. Soon, dozens of Russian soldiers started shooting anything in Ruska Lozova that looked like an electronic device: cell towers, CCTV cameras, and even building intercoms with integrated cameras. They were certain that they were being watched by American intelligence officers, who were sitting comfortably in front of their monitors, cup of coffee in hand. Back then, all communications between Russian soldiers travelled on unprotected lines; even I could listen in to orders being given on a basic radio. No one needed the CIA to locate those groups of young Russian soldiers and aim a cannon at them.

One day, in Ruska Lozova, a lady with cancer walked up to a uniformed lieutenant and tugged on his sleeve. "I've finished my palliative medication. Either go get me some in Russia, or let me go buy it in Kharkiv (which was under Kyiv's control). Soon I'll be screaming in pain and it won't stop; I'll follow you around wherever you go, screaming." The lieutenant turned to her and said, "I'm a terrorist. I don't do things like that."

Many of the Russian soldiers grew up in poverty, and when they saw houses larger than their own, with appliances and computers they could never afford, their frustration and paranoia turned to envy. They started breaking into homes and apartments, tore washing machines out of the walls, and loaded them onto military trucks. They stole hair straighteners to bring to their girlfriends. "Naturally, they stole bottles of vodka, but they also took perfume bottles that were only a third full, or already opened boxes of chocolates," Nykola told me. The final days of the occupation, when they knew the Ukrainian counteroffensive was close by, were the worst. They set fire to the house of a man with whom they had argued, killing three members of his family. They executed another man because he had concealed a rifle from them, which he used to shoot birds for food. The day before the Ukrainian soldiers arrived, the gardens of small detached houses were filled with graves. "They killed out of frustration, to punish us for defeating them, and maybe even to avenge the unnecessary deaths of their comrades."

Evident in the trivial and yet deadly mistakes Moscow made at the beginning of the war, and in the chaos they caused beyond the front line, is a lack of respect for their own soldiers and for the mission itself. An anecdote I heard while en route to Kherson really brings home this point.

The loss of Kherson in the south represents an unforgettable defeat for the Russian army, as it was the only regional capital they managed to conquer. On November 11, 2022, two days after the Russian retreat, the sun shone brightly in a clear blue sky, and the temperature was surprisingly warm for November in Ukraine. Celebration was in the air, it felt like the town had won an important soccer match: people strolled by in groups, smiling and knocking on people's windows. People whistled as they walked. Drivers beeped their horns. Youngsters zipped by on scooters, waving flags. Watermelons, the city's emblem, were everywhere. Two young people, wrapped in a European Union flag, kissed passionately in Freedom Square, the center of the celebration. Countless flags—both the Ukrainian one and that of the EU—fluttered in the place where Lenin's statue once stood.

The resistance movement in Kherson made world news, as did the Russian army's eventual defeat. For more than eight months, Moscow had occupied the city, with Putin annexing it to the Russian Federation by decree only six weeks earlier. But when the soldiers started their retreat, one of their commanders, Oleg Zubkov, focused on something else entirely: he decided to steal a raccoon, a llama, and a monkey from the Kherson zoo.

Zubkov is a fan of exotic animals and started his own safari park in Crimea called Taigan. In his profile photo on social media, he is seen riding a lion. While he was struggling to catch the raccoon, who put up a fight, holding onto a branch with all four paws, Commander Zubkov ordered his subordinates to take a video of him to post on his social media. The men, already humiliated and defeated in war, felt insulted by this Russian military blogger who had hundreds of thousands of followers on Telegram. But Zubkov was successful; he managed to detach the raccoon from its branch, threw it in a cage, and carted it off.

The commander is a vain man who once managed to avoid house arrest thanks to personal connections. There, too, his conviction was related to his passion for wild animals: a lion he owned attacked a small child, who later had to have their finger amputated. The judge gave him two years and three months in prison, but the Supreme Court of occupied Crimea overturned the sentence. In 2020, he found himself on trial again after yet another park visitor was attacked by one of his lions, but once more, he escaped punishment because the leader of Crimea, Sergej Aksyonov, named by Putin himself, vouched for him.

During the occupation's coldest months, Commander Zubkov's men, like the Ukrainian citizens of Kherson, went hungry. The reason for their retreat was essentially that they could no longer receive supplies; access routes from Crimea had been cut off. This constituted a major military problem for the Russian soldiers. They could no longer receive shipments of weapons, reinforcements, or ammunition. Moreover, they no longer had a solid escape route. They also lacked food, which theoretically exists in abundance in Kherson. After all, this area has the most fertile soil in Ukraine and is dotted with farms, but farmland requires upkeep if it is to bear fruit. The province was also home to the largest poultry farm in all of Europe—a monstrous establishment that housed four million adult hens and roosters, and seven hundred thousand chicks. When the Ukrainian army returned to Kherson, they discovered close to five million decomposing chickens, dead for months, constituting a major health and hygiene hazard. Instead of working on the farm and using it to feed the inhabitants and their own soldiers, the Russians had abandoned it. While the chickens starved to death, while soldiers went hungry, and during a crushing defeat that will long be remembered, Commander Zubkov was focused solely on increasing his fan base via his YouTube channel and adding new videos, such as the one where he jogs alongside a recently stolen llama named Roma.

For a long time, Anna Politkovskaya was considered by Europe to be a brilliant, courageous, and extremely talented

Russian journalist who was too skeptical about Russia and its future. And then we realized that everything we've seen and learned about Russia during the invasion of Ukraine had already been described for us in her books. As the months went by, I realized that every anecdote I heard—every heartbreaking soldier's story, every sacrilegious and unpunished action by an officer—reminded me of the first chapter of *Putin's Russia* by Anna Politkovskaya.

> The Army in Russia is a closed system no different from a prison. Nobody gets into the Army or into prison unless the authorities want them there. Once you are in, you live the life of a slave . . . When [Putin] first appeared on Russia's political radar screen as a possible head of state . . . he began by making pronouncements to the effect that the Army . . . was henceforth to be reborn, and that all that it lacked for its renaissance was a second Chechen war . . . . When the Second Chechen War started, the Army was given free rein, and in the presidential elections of 2000 it voted as one for Putin. The Army has found the present war highly profitable . . . . How exactly Putin has helped the Army we shall see in the stories that follow. You can decide for yourself whether you would like to live in a country where your taxes sustain such an institution. How would you feel when your sons turned 18 and were conscripted as "human resources." How satisfied you would be with an Army from which soldiers deserted in droves every week, sometimes whole squads or entire companies at a time. What would you think of an Army in which, in a single year, 2002, a battalion, more than 500 men, had been killed not fighting a war but from beatings? In which the officers stole everything from the 10-rouble notes sent to privates by their parents to entire tank columns?[32]

Pavel, a parachutist who fought for two months with the

56th paratrooper regiment, which was once an elite unit to which his father had also belonged, shared a thick dossier of notes and photos—141 pages detailing his life as a Russian soldier in Ukraine in 2022—on the social network VKontakte. The file describes a military universe in a rapid state of decline. Corrupt colonels steal rations from their troops, then try and resell kits containing energy bars, protein powder, and vitamin drinks on eBay. During training, paratroopers can't jump more than once a day because too many of them haven't learned how to fold their 60-meter square silk parachutes yet; they take too long, and the sun goes down. When the cold weather sets in, they have to wait weeks for winter jackets. Combat boots arrive, but not in the right sizes. At one point, there's an outbreak of Covid on the base, but instead of treating the soldiers, their superiors falsify the test results.

Pavel is certain that Putin's army had far fewer than the two hundred thousand soldiers they said it did at the beginning of the invasion. He believes that the corruption and falsification are so rampant that even the people in the war office at the Kremlin don't really know how many men are on the ground.

"We need bodies. That's why you were brought here," a group of men were reportedly told after they'd been rounded up in Voronezh, a city in western Russia, and brought to the front during a deployment called by Putin in September 2022. On hearing this, fifty of them decided to escape from the front and return to Russia. They marched one hundred twenty-six kilometers on foot, weapons in hand. They were then captured, disarmed, imprisoned, and blackmailed until they agreed to return to fight.[33]

In early November, a group of girlfriends, mothers, teenage daughters, and wives travelled by car to the border to retrieve their men. At the training center in Zaitseve, the girls were met by armed guards. Having no other recourse available to them, the women filmed a video denouncing the situation and uploaded it to the web. In the video, they're all wearing windbreakers, their faces are white with cold, and they stand motionless in front of the camera.[34] One of them stands in the middle, reading from a piece of paper, articulating every word very carefully. Their men, she says, were taken on October 1 and were sent, without any training, to defend the occupied territories in Luhansk after only ten days. There, she goes on to say, they were abandoned by their officers, who stayed in their barracks, and sent to fight without knowing how. On November 1, they were transported to a location near Svatove, where the battle was raging, and told to dig trenches. It was night, and they were exposed to enemy fire. All they had were machine guns, which were of no use, not when the Ukrainians were bombarding them with long-range artillery and drones.

The girl goes on to remind President Putin of what he had promised—that inexperienced soldiers who had just been recruited would not be sent to the front line. "Why weren't they trained? Why were they abandoned by their officers? Why were they at the front, where they shouldn't have been, without the proper equipment?" Then she pauses, raises her eyes from the piece of paper, and looks straight into the camera, as do her companions. "We call on you to remove our men and sons from this hell."

For twenty years, Vladimir Putin told us that he had the second most powerful army in the world, while Politkovskaya continued to depict it as a broken system, cruel to its soldiers, inefficient, vaunted, and overhyped. We believed Putin. Before she was killed in her Moscow apartment building elevator, bags of groceries in her hands, she wrote: "Russia is about to fall into an abyss dug by Putin and his political short-sightedness."[35]

I met Vera Politkovskaya, Anna's daughter, on the first anniversary of Putin's full-scale invasion of Ukraine. Vera is a journalist, but says that Russian journalism is dead. She stayed in Moscow after her mother was killed, but fled after the beginning of the war on Ukraine. We talked about a beautiful movie that came out in 1991, *A Taste of Freedom*. The movie is about her father, not her mother, although she is present in the background. At the time, her mother was not yet the well-known journalist, but a young woman "with a carefree nature that few people saw, but already with the distinct gaze and character everyone would come to recognize." After her assassination, a second movie was released entirely about her: *A Bitter Taste of Freedom*.

We talked about the pseudo-religious sects that popped up like mushrooms when the Soviet Union dissolved, about people's ravenous hunger for anything mystical after years of government-imposed secularism, with all its shortcomings. We talked about the "wild 1990s," a period that Putin considers a disgrace to his "empire," and which she, on the other hand, considers the last time people in Russia were able to think freely. The space that was created after the collapse of the Soviet Union and before the era of Putin was chaotic, and because of that, freer and more exciting: "It was the last time we Russians could envision the future ahead of us, with all its possibilities. No, today there's no space left where it is possible to cultivate a free conscience in Russia."

We talked about the Putin of today, the Russians of today, and about nuclear weapons. We talked about her daughter, who, like mother and grandmother, cannot lie, either to herself or to others. After expressing her thoughts on the Ukraine war in her high school classroom, Vera's daughter was betrayed in the worst way possible—by her schoolmates. After that came the death threats. At that point, Vera, who despite having lost so much to Moscow believed she could withstand anything, packed up her books and things and fled with her daughter.

After Anna's assassination in 2006, Vera chose to stay—because she didn't want to upset her daughter's world any further, because she had her own work as a journalist, and because she wanted to fight for justice for her mother. She needed to be present for the investigations, to make sure they wouldn't lead to dead ends or follow false leads. But after February 24, 2022, her feelings changed. "Any support that Putin had before the invasion turned into support for the war after it. When I realized this, I became aware that I could no longer do my job in Russia. My last name—which has been forgotten in my own country—suddenly resurfaced, and in the most dangerous way possible, as the name of an internal enemy." Life is harder for a traitor during times of war than during peace. "What happened to my daughter at school is proof of this; that's what convinced me to leave."

We talked about the nameless Russian soldiers—the "bodies" that had been "needed," people who had been killed but were never looked for, never identified, never returned to their families—that had obsessed her mother. Anna had told their stories, which were their mothers' stories about the bureaucratic odysseys they undertook to try and find out what had happened to their sons' corpses.

Russian propaganda often claims that the Russian people are not afraid of dying, while Europeans and Americans are, and that this makes us in the West fundamentally weaker. Putin draws on this premise to suggest that, although victory may take time, the Russian people will ultimately prevail, because they are willing to sacrifice themselves to reach their goal—unlike Europeans, who are considered unable to see things through. The idea is that Europe will grow tired of Kyiv and abandon it, while Russia will continue to sacrifice its men, as it did in the wars against Napoleon and Hitler.

I asked Vera if she thought that the Russians of today, in 2023, have that same spirit of sacrifice, the tendency to obey, the courage to die.

"That's not an easy question."

"This time around," I say, "it's not just about defending your homes from Napoleon or Hitler; it's about dying for lands that have been devastated and abandoned, wastelands, something that you, as citizens of the largest country in the world, already have in abundance."

"Yes, the tragic irony is that tens of thousands of Russians are dying to conquer something that we already have, and that we don't know what to do with: endless tracts of land. Because that is exactly what Russia is trying to obtain from Ukraine. Even though the longer this war lasts, the less Moscow gains from it, and even though it is a senseless war, your question is still very difficult to answer. Without a doubt, Russians are a proud people, capable of making enormous sacrifices. And while a Russian man may have a hard time explaining why he should die for this cause, Putin still stands a chance of winning—as long as he continues to send Russian soldiers and civilians to die in Ukraine. Actually, I wouldn't bet on Russians being the ones to end the war."

When Vera was still a child, Anna Politkovskaya would come home from trips to Chechnya, where she went to report on the war there, with a cloth backpack full of human bones.

They were the bones of simple soldiers without rank or name, "The men who may not have been afraid of dying." They were the men who no one ever had any intention of counting, identifying, returning to their loved ones, and finally burying. Anna used to pile them up under her desk and say, "If I have their bones, they're no longer ghosts."

Part Three: Afghanistan

V.
Ghosts

Born in Afghanistan in 1994, Zarifa Ghafari grew up thinking that one day she would go into politics; it was still possible when she became an adult. In 2021, however, everything changed.

Slender with smooth skin, Zarifa has almond-shaped eyes and prefers a white veil to a black one. In 2018, at the age of twenty-four, she's the youngest mayor in the country, in Maidan Shar. Part of the road she has to take to work every day, some of which cuts through the desert and some through fields, is controlled by the Taliban. Her driver hits the accelerator when they pass through that area, his left hand firmly on the wheel, a gun in his right. Zarifa spent her teenage years organizing marches, hanging protest banners, taking part in rallies, and arguing with men. That Afghanistan now seems very remote, but actually the 2010s were not that long ago. "It was difficult back then, but at least it was possible," she says.[36] At the time, she had two key slogans, which she shouted into a megaphone either from the street or from a small stage erected in the sand: "One year of educated girls will save ten generations of Afghans," and "Men had their chance for fifty years, and failed."

The Taliban send her threatening letters. One says, "You're helping democracy, and spreading vice among our people!" Of all the cruel phrases included in the threats she has received over the years, "You're helping democracy," intended as an insult—as if it were emblematic of all sinners and sins—remains engraved in her memory. That same letter concludes a few lines later with: "Stop what you are doing within one week, or we will kill you."

She received that letter in 2017. In 2020, Zarifa reread it with a smile: "I'm still alive!" Not long after, on a Sunday in March, four armed men opened fire on her jeep. "They tried to assassinate me three times, and when they failed, they killed my father." Zarifa's father was a military man; the day the Americans arrived in 2001, he immediately went to the barber to have the long beard he had been forced to wear under the Islamist regime cut off. He had always hated the beard; it made him feel unkempt and untidy, he found it undignified, and it did not reflect his careful style or manner.

Even though she was only seven years old in 2001, Zarifa recalls him coming home clean-shaven. It wasn't just the lack of beard that was different, though. For the first time, he had a relaxed expression on his face. "I think I inherited his obsessive-compulsive tendencies," Zarifa says, alluding to their shared need to bring order where there is chaos, to fix things that are broken, and to repair injustices.

In 2001, Zarifa's father had not shaved in six years, since the Taliban had—partially and almost by accident—conquered Afghanistan. Although their leader, Mullah Omar, had never been known for his military prowess, in 1996, he knew how to take advantage of the circumstances.

Before the West invaded Afghanistan, there hadn't been peace; there had been a civil war between mujahideen. The Taliban were the fundamentalist faction, and although the majority of the population did not support them and were in fact terrified of them, the majority was fragmented. Meanwhile, the soldiers and civilians who backed Mullah Omar were united and obedient in a way that only the most extreme, radical forces tend to be.

When the Americans arrived, the conflict did not unfold in the usual way: Mullah Omar and his men did not even try and defend the capital. They fled. After the American troops on the ground—which were relatively few—and their numerous local allies took control of Afghanistan, the guerrilla phase of the war began, one that would last twenty years. The most diehard Taliban fighters drove car bombs into foreign soldiers, who in turn launched special operations to flush the Taliban out of their hiding places.

Zarifa also recalls the time her father had told her in a whisper that he had always prayed to God for a daughter. "It's hard to explain to foreigners how strange and rare it was back then for an Afghan father to wish for a daughter, and in fact, I still haven't found the right words to express it." Unable to punish her, the Taliban struck out at her father, and not only as a way of getting back at her, but also because they considered him equally as guilty, and perhaps even more so. In a system where girls are considered ghosts, responsibility for all events weighs solely on the shoulders of men; Zarifa's father had committed the crime of raising a free woman.

Zarifa's grandmother had been a factory worker. Zarifa's mother had gone to school and was also involved in politics. The idea that the laws currently in effect in the country are the formalized version of widely shared cultural practices is a Western misconception—one that is contradicted by countless Afghan family histories.

Before being essentially excluded from the labor market, women contributed one billion dollars to the country's GDP. These days, female medical students who have passed their exams cannot graduate and become doctors, which means that they cannot assist the tens of thousands of Afghan patients who are often abandoned by the emirate's impoverished and debilitated healthcare system. Preventing these women from receiving their degrees also means that a time will come when there will be no more female doctors in a country where it is frowned upon for a woman to undress in front of a doctor she does not know, a country where some husbands do not allow their wives to be treated by male doctors.

In 2020, nineteen years after the arrival of foreign military forces, the mortality rates of mothers and newborns had decreased to less than a third of what they were at the end of the first Taliban emirate in 2001. In a country where "pregnancy and childbirth have killed far more women and babies than bombs and bullets," as Zarifa often says, her battle cry of "One year of educated girls will save ten generations of Afghans" is far more than a poetic slogan. Depriving Afghanistan's struggling hospitals of hundreds of female doctors does not just hurt the emancipated women of Afghanistan—it also harms the traditionalist women who never even contemplated removing their burkas, Afghan children, adult males, and the Taliban soldiers themselves, all of whom could have been treated by those young women.

In 2014, the United Nations started a project to train five thousand Afghan policewomen. Today, by contrast, the ISKP—an acronym for Islamic State Khorasan Province, now the most common name for the Islamic State of Afghanistan—spreads terror throughout the country at the rate of one attack a week. Terrorists show up in crowded mosques during Friday prayers, or at the front door of the Ministry of Foreign Affairs in downtown Kabul, disguised as women, concealing bombs under their burkas.

The Taliban are all men, and men are not allowed to search women. When I crossed over into Afghanistan by foot along the northern border from Uzbekistan, via the Soviet-built Friendship Bridge, at the very first checkpoint, I encountered a young man with a rifle who had just come on duty. He had the task of checking my entry documents. He looked at my passport but never once looked me in the eye; I could easily have been someone other than the person in the photo. When it came time to check my backpack for dangerous or illegal items, he opened the zipper, came across a bra strap, and quickly shut it again without searching further. Eyes cast downward, he waved me on. I could've hidden anything in that backpack, including explosives.

Because the Taliban is not allowed to look under burkas, which would allow it to find Islamic State bombs, and since there's no female police force or security agents, explosives circulate freely in Afghanistan, killing men, women, children, and members of the Taliban. Essentially, the humanitarian crisis and the terrorist emergency, the two dramatic situations that characterize the post-war period in Afghanistan, are due, in part, to the fact that half the population is excluded from having a role in the country.

In one year of Taliban rule, terrorist attacks by the Islamic State killed a thousand Afghans. "For now, the blood that has been spilled is our own, but soon the West will be forced to deal with the Islamic State," Zarifa declares severely.

Panic

We hear the sound of gunshot. The hotel is being attacked. They hit six bedroom windows between the fourth and seventh floors. The glass is double-glazed, bulletproof. The windows crack, but do not shatter. I'm on a Skype call with the Rome studios of La7, an Italian television channel. Someone knocks at the door, a man tells me to take cover, I go back to the computer screen and gently explain that I have to interrupt the call—my instinct tells me to slam the laptop shut and run. The studio realizes something is happening: "Show us." We need to move quickly away from the balcony, lock ourselves in the bathroom, and wait for instructions regarding the possible evacuation of the hotel, how and where we should go. If no one breaks in, we're safer from gunshot on the lower floors, because there's a wall around the building. We head downstairs.

Another, more dangerous, hypothesis is that the bullets

hitting the windows are not collateral damage from a skirmish taking place out on the streets, but the initial phase of the storming of the hotel. The Islamic State might be preparing to attack the building; it's full of Westerners, foreign journalists on their laptops, and UN agency employees. If this is the case, all floors are equally unsafe.

The Star Hotel in Kabul is inside the Green Zone, a neighborhood full of embassies and international organizations. It's always been the safest area in the city, but it no longer is: the embassies have recently been evacuated, and even the soldiers who once defended them are already on board military flights heading home.

The possibility that this is an attack on the hotel is considered probable for all of ten minutes. It then becomes clear that this is not an operation organized by the same terrorist group that killed one hundred seventy Afghan citizens and thirteen American soldiers in a suicide attack at Hamid Karzai International Airport a few days earlier, on August 26, 2021. The shots being fired in the air, but not quite high enough, are the Taliban's desperate attempt to frighten and disperse the young women and men out marching in the streets, who are protesting against them, the coup d'état that allowed the Taliban to regain power, and the "Pakistani invasion" of Afghanistan—and in favor of women's rights and the very fragile armed resistance currently going on in Panjshir province.

On September 3, 2021, a WhatsApp group called "Powerful Women" was created by twenty-seven-year-old Ramzia Abdekhil and some friends, many of whom prefer to remain anonymous and protect their identities by using virtual profiles with imaginative nicknames composed of letters and emoticons. "Powerful Women" hold their protest rallies in a different location each day to prevent the Taliban from stopping them from congregating, and then eventually make their way into the center of the city. Among the protesters are thousands of female high school students who never had to live under

Taliban rules and who, up until just recently, imagined futures for themselves that are now incompatible with the new laws of the Islamic Emirate. These girls wear gauzy white veils and school uniforms. Protesters also include journalists from the Rukhshana collective, many of whom decided not to get married when it was still possible for them to work and make a living without needing a man to survive. But on August 15, 2021, everything changed. "All I can do now is fight," one of them tells me. "Even if I wanted to submit to the regime to survive, who would marry a girl like me in Taliban Afghanistan?"

Members also include women who were sold by their families when they were still children to violent and much older men. During the two decades of the Republic, many of these women were able to obtain divorces from judges after offering proof of the abuse they had suffered. The Taliban, however, does not recognize those pieces of paper that set the women free, and now they're terrified that they'll be forced to return to their torturers.

Part of the group is a woman judge who, some years ago, sentenced many Taliban members to several years in prison for planting car bombs around the city. Now that those men are in power, they can take their revenge on her. "They've taken over the Ministry of Justice and the courts. They can easily find out where I live. My particular situation is rare: I'm in less danger out demonstrating than shut inside my own apartment."

The WhatsApp group "Powerful Women" offers its members clear instructions on how to stay safe. One of the messages from the administrators says: "Wear a surgical mask, keep your veil on your head, and wear dark sunglasses. Don't do anything foolish. Don't take any unnecessary risks. Don't let anyone recognize you."

Safety measures such as these did not manage to protect all the members of the network. In September 2021, two girls from Herat, a large city in the west that until a few days earlier had been under the control of the Italian military, were shot and killed by the Taliban while protesting. In November, in Mazar-i-Sharif, the body of twenty-year-old activist, Frozan Safi, was found without documents along an expressway. Even the two most prominent activists in the group, Tamana Paryani and Parwana Ibrahim Khil, disappeared in January 2022.

The day that the Taliban announce the formation of their government to the world begins with the men shooting and beating the protesters with their rifle butts. It ends with the Taliban spokesman, Zabiullah Mujahid, telling the press who will cover which roles. The position of interim prime minister goes to Mullah Hasan Akhund, who is on the United Nations terrorist list and who was the deputy prime minister of the Taliban twenty years ago. His right-hand man is Mullah Baradar, one of the Taliban founders, the political leader of the so-called "moderate wing," and the man who negotiated a peace treaty with the Americans—which is to say Donald Trump's administration—in Doha. In charge of Defense is ex-leader Mullah Omar's son, Mohammad Yaqoob. But the most shocking appointment of all is that of Minister of the Interior; the man responsible for making sure Afghans follow the rules and for assuring their safety is Sirajuddin Haqqani, a good friend of the Al Qaeda terrorist group, a wanted man, and the head of the maximalist wing of the party. For anyone who ever believed—besides the American administration—their promise of creating a government that included women and ethnic minorities (in a country where there is no ethnic majority, where they're all minorities, with the Pashtun, the source of the Taliban, being the largest), this clearly does not constitute an inclusive government.

Don't mistake the postwar period for peace

"Make no mistake: this is the Biden agenda," House Speaker Nancy Pelosi said in a conversation with the editor of *The Atlantic*, Jeffrey Goldberg, six weeks after Kabul returned to Taliban hands on August 15, 2021.[37] The day the last American soldier left Afghanistan, the army checkpoints in the capital's Green Zone were taken over by members of the Haqqani clan. One Afghan UN official called them the "hardline faction" but never actually named them, showing both deference to and fear of the new regime. He wasn't even sure if he himself had the right to leave the country—or whether, even then, it would have been possible in practice: "Even if you are on the evacuation list of a Western country . . . it's patently clear to us that there isn't room for everyone." The official didn't even know if he should show up for work the next day. "The system password on my institutional laptop doesn't work anymore." He wasn't sure he still had a job: "Is the United Nations withdrawing from Afghanistan, too?"

The Haqqani group is financed by the Pakistani secret service and has had a long relationship with Al Qaeda. It's a clan: Sirajuddin's father was one of Osama bin Laden's mentors; bin Laden's successor, Ayman al Zawahiri, was killed one year after retiring, in August 2022, by an American drone in an apartment owned by the Haqqani group in the upscale Sherpur neighborhood of Kabul. Joe Biden commented on the operation using words he often repeated during the 2021 evacuation to justify the disaster: "I simply do not believe that the safety and security of America is enhanced by continuing to deploy thousands of American troops . . . We just don't need to fight a ground war to do it . . . . We have what's called over-the-horizon capabilities, which means we can strike terrorists and targets without American boots on the ground—or very few, if needed."[38] The strike against al Zawahiri was a success; the one prior to it had an unclear outcome; the one before that killed ten Afghan civilians, seven of whom were children, instead of the Islamic State battalion that was supposed to be the target.

A number of observers, US war veterans, and politicians have wondered how al Zawahiri managed to live in a terraced penthouse in the center of Kabul (the CIA had been observing him for at least four months), keep a regular routine, and go out in broad daylight, all very risky for a wanted criminal. Why wasn't he hiding in a cave in the mountains on the border with Pakistan, like the Taliban once did?

The tribal regions of the Nangarhar mountains along the border are Haqqani territory. It was there that, thirty years ago, Saudi terrorist Osama bin Laden met with Egyptian terrorist al Zawahiri for the first time. It was there that, a decade later, they planned the attack on the Twin Towers and the Pentagon. It was from there that they had to flee in 2001, when the United States invaded Afghanistan.

In 2022, al Zawahiri could step freely out onto his balcony each morning because he had a friend and protector in the government—Minister of the Interior Haqqani, himself a wanted man with a ten million dollar bounty on his head.

On August 16, 2021, Biden said: "Our mission in Afghanistan was never supposed to have been nation building."[39] Their goal had been to punish and render the Al Qaeda network harmless. The Taliban do not want global jihad—they're nationalists—but they have a habit of allowing their terrorist allies, whose goals extend beyond the country's borders, to prosper, make plans, and move freely around the country, as we have seen with Al Qaeda. However, they're not effective at containing enemy groups with similar goals—groups who have declared war on the Taliban government. In fact, as soon as the Taliban returned to power, the ISKP's ranking began to climb on *al Naba*, the official gazette of the Islamic State. This list tracks various groups located in Arab, African, and Asian countries where the organization is present, with the ranking based on how many "infidels" are killed and how many successful operations are carried out.

The Islamic State's preferred targets are members of the Hazara community, even more than authority figures or foreign (and particularly Chinese) delegations. The Hazara are one of the many minorities that make up multiethnic Afghanistan, and they count for 15-20% of the total population. The Taliban, Al Qaeda, and the Islamic State are all Sunni fundamentalists; they consider the Hazara Shiite community a group of heretical traitors. Before the Islamic State started persecuting them, the Hazara community was persecuted by the Taliban. These days, the safety of the Shiites is not a priority: in one year alone, the Islamic State killed seven hundred Hazara men, women, and children with suicide attacks in mosques, by gunning down laborers on their way to work, and with car bombs in the marketplace. Hundreds of thousands of Hazara have fled across the western border into Iran in search of protection, where they have found it.

Back in 2003, Biden said the opposite of what he said on 16 August 2021, namely: "The alternative to nation-building in Afghanistan is chaos; it is in chaos that drug traffickers and international terrorists thrive."[40] At the heart of the Doha agreement, the peace treaty between the United States and the Taliban signed in early 2020 during the Trump administration, one clause stood out in particular. A guarantee. Afghanistan promised it would not offer hospitality to the global jihad. The assassination of al Zawahiri, carried out in 2022 by the CIA in Kabul, proves that the Taliban lied about what truly mattered to the Americans—not to mention everything that directly regarded the lives of Afghans.

Deception

The presence of Haqqani's soldiers at the checkpoints during the evacuations presented a serious problem: they recognized all the men of the recently collapsed Republic, which is to say, the people who desperately needed to be saved. The "hardline faction" never accepted the internationally accepted rule of sparing allies and partners. Italian GIS soldiers (a special unit of the Carabinieri), the Italian 9th assault regiment "Col

Moschin," the British forces, and the Australians left the airport perimeter, where evacuations were taking place, and went into the city to rescue Afghan partners and female parliamentarians, magistrates, and mayors like Zarifa Ghafari, for whom it was dangerous to proceed through Taliban checkpoints on their own. Initially, the Americans didn't want to partake in these rescue operations and tried to prevent their colleagues from doing so; as a result, there were a number of serious arguments between exhausted commanders of the allied units.

Soldiers from Italy and other members of the international coalition searched the city of Kabul for the men and women they had worked with for years. Around August 20, an American commander stationed at the Abbey Gate checkpoint at Hamid Karzai International Airport told them to cease all such activity: they were making widespread evacuation seem like a possibility and making the US contingent look bad, as they were forced to follow frustrating and severe rules of engagement. It was forbidden to actively search for people whose names were on priority lists, to leave the gate area, and to interact directly with the Taliban.

Some of the people on those lists, while trying to reach the airport on their own, were forced to make deals with Taliban leaders—handing over the keys to their houses and cars, or offering them bags containing a hundred thousand dollars in cash, or both. Later, they discovered that none of these deals were valid for the Haqqani clan. This happened to Aziz Amin Ahmadzai, the former president's personal secretary, for example.

In the Green Zone, the men of the clan were immediately recognizable for how jumpy they were, and for how they never looked women in the face. A joke, both cruel and telling, circulated among Western journalists at the Star Hotel: "Joe Biden and the Taliban have one thing in common: every night they pray for the day when Afghanistan will stop appearing on the front page of newspapers." During the third week of August 2021, the curve that measured President Biden's approval rating (as calculated by FiveThirtyEight, a US polling aggregation website discontinued in 2024) intersected with his disapproval rating, with the latter overtaking the former. It stayed that way for the rest of his presidency.

For the Taliban, from a political point of view, this was the moment of the "big lie," when the priority was money, not burkas. They urgently needed to deceive the international community about their real intentions in order to unfreeze government assets—seven billion dollars of the Afghan Central Bank were held by the Federal Reserve in New York, and two billion dollars were in European banks. This represented the second-largest freeze of sanctioned assets worldwide, after Iran in 1980.

The Taliban understood that, for as long as Afghanistan remained at the center of attention, they had to lie. "People who helped the previous government—the Americans and their allies—will be spared." "Women who work and study will definitely be allowed to continue doing so." "We are not going to force women to wear burkas." "We have changed." These were all promises made by spokesman Zabiullah Mujahid from the stage of the large circular hall in the Ministry of Information during press conferences broadcast live, in their entirety, by networks as diverse as *Al Jazeera* and the *BBC*.

People stopped believing the big lie when, on August 23, the Taliban went over the top. In an interview with *Newsweek*, a representative of the Cultural Commission, Abdul Qahar Balkhi, asked that the government of the Islamic Emirate be immediately recognized by the entire international community and managed to make a heretofore unthought of mockery of public opinion when he said, "We believe the world has a unique opportunity of rapprochement and coming together to tackle the challenges not only facing us but the entire humanity," with these challenges including "world security" and "climate change."[41]

The (not so fast) end of an era

In July 2021, when the Taliban were still an armed rebel group and another group was legitimately governing Kabul, the Chinese Foreign Minister, Wang Yi, officially met a Taliban delegation led by the head of the Political Commission, Abdul Ghani Baradar, in Tianjin, northern China. The purpose was not related to business. China did not need the American withdrawal to make gains in Afghanistan; even before the meeting, it was under contract to manage almost all the country's mines and oversee the extraction of rare minerals. The joy shown by Xi Jinping and Vladimir Putin after the collapse of Kabul on August 15, 2021, was insincere: for Russia and China, the Afghan disaster was dangerously close to their borders, and in the case of China, actually touched them. But it was also the perfect occasion to gloat over the American failure, elevating it to an "end of an era" status—which made it worth all the trouble.

It's hard to forget certain images from those days: the Taliban entering the Arg; Westerners panicking and fleeing; Afghans grabbing onto the wings and wheels of US aircraft, desperate to escape; the twentieth anniversary of the attack on the Twin Towers on September 11, with correspondents from the world's main television stations reporting live from Kabul, the American embassy behind them now draped in a gigantic Taliban flag. All of these constituted unrepeatable moments of jubilation for Putin and Xi.

The Chinese press immediately took advantage of the moment to remind Taiwan that an alliance with the United States has its limits, that they were better off not trusting Washington. The Kremlin began to fantasize that—in case of a full-scale invasion of Ukraine, which would effectively take place six months later—the West's support for Kyiv would be weak and temporary.

In Italy, there was much discussion of how the combined strength of Kyiv and its allies might "provoke" the Russian president to act with extreme violence, when, in actual fact, Putin's army showed maximum violence at the outset of the war, in March 2022, against the city of Mariupol, and not after significant Western military aid began to flow into Ukraine, in June 2022. From that moment forward, the Ukrainians and their territory were considerably better defended; the damage and ruthlessness of Russian operations did not increase.

Looking back at a timeline of events, it makes sense to wonder if the exact opposite is true: that a show of Western weakness, and not strength, triggered the Russian president's violent expansionist dreams. The disastrous withdrawal from Kabul and the entire failure in Afghanistan were a prelude to war in Ukraine, and led Putin to think that the time was right to act on a twisted plan he had been mulling over for years. While the Russian president had already staged a number of simulations in the past, he had never actually given the order to begin. In August 2021, Putin saw Kyiv as a failed state, with the countries that could have potentially helped it now defeated, in retreat, and no longer strong enough or willing to make costly and long-term commitments beyond their borders.

They must have thought that the West was tired, the belief in the end of American hegemony clouding their facts. Russia and China are stockpiling vast quantities of weapons—generally less sophisticated, part of a less efficient organizational framework—but they're short of strong allies. *Financial Times* columnist John Lloyd put a stop to the wave of anti-Western schadenfreude:

> The Soviet Union had a protective wall of communist-run states to the west and north—now these states (with

the partial exception of Hungary) are distrustful or hostile. China inspires fear not affection in its region, and while its neo-colonial expansion through the Belt and Road creates joint projects with cash-strapped states like Italy and Greece, neither country would prefer life in a China-dominated community of nations to their present membership of the EU.[42]

In short, it's encouraging, but not surprising, that countries used to living in a democracy would choose it over other systems. This choice—which is never questioned despite the unforgivable blunders, crimes, and errors committed by the Americans and other free countries around the world—is the long-term guarantee of the power of democracy.

And yet, we should never forget our mistakes. In *Can Intervention Work?*, Rory Stewart and Gerald Knaus anticipated the collapse of Afghanistan without being overly fatalistic or denouncing the decadence of the West.[43] Published in 2011, the book examines the mishaps of that period with a straightforward premise: Afghanistan can exist without the Taliban. It is not condemned, by history or destiny, to suffer forever. The outcome was disastrous because of a long series of avoidable mistakes.

"The French were responsible for their own Revolution"

While the French people managed to bring about their own Revolution, the Italians needed outside help to be liberated from fascism. One of the reasons the Italian Resistance was successful was that they were not alone in fighting the enemy; foreign powers, with far more robust military means than what the clandestine partisans had, fought fascism alongside them.

Ever since Vladimir Putin attempted to conquer the capital of a country that did not want him, and then tried to kill that country's democratically elected president in February 2022, a theory has taken root in Italy that sees Ukraine—engaged in a war against Russian invasion—in the right, and yet, if Italy were to step in and help Ukraine instead of remaining neutral, it would end up in the wrong. The theory posits that the Ukrainians should fend for themselves and that it would actually be better if they didn't fight at all. Neither the Italian partisans nor the French revolutionaries believed the slogan, "Better red than dead." On the contrary, the French motto "Liberty or death!" was sung in the streets and sewn onto flags during the French Revolution, which in turn led to contemporary democracy.

The same people who today remind the Ukrainians "Better red than dead," accused the Afghans, in relatively recent August 2021, of not fighting back against the Taliban forcefully enough. In that moment, accusing the Afghans of being defeatists served as a way to blame the Americans. The argument went like this: Washington had imposed certain liberties and a lifestyle on a population that neither needed nor wanted them, did not recognize them as their own, and therefore did not defend them.

But was this really the case? Can we be sure that the Afghans did not appreciate their new rights? The hundreds of thousands of girls and young women who filled Afghan schools and universities were sent there by their families, not by the Americans. During the six elections that took place in Afghanistan between 2001 and 2021, Afghans went and voted freely—despite the fact that the Taliban planted car bombs at polling stations and threatened to kill anyone who collected a ballot—and were not accompanied to the polls at gunpoint by foreign soldiers.

The number of Afghans who died fighting the Taliban far surpasses the number of Western soldiers who died in the entire mission that began in 2001, so why didn't Afghan soldiers defend Kabul in the summer of 2021? The most common answer—that the majority of Afghans appreciate the Taliban, and that the West imposed certain freedoms on them—is not the most truthful.

To begin with, the Taliban descend from the Pashtun ethnic group, which is not the majority in Afghanistan. Many other ethnic groups (as well as a number of Pashtuns) abhor the Emirate that was forced on them by the Taliban: it does not resemble or represent them; they want their present and future to be different. Then, and this is critical, there's the fact of how exactly the Taliban returned to power.

The Doha pact between the United States and the Taliban excluded the Afghan government, allied with the West, from the negotiations, and contained a series of written clauses and secret verbal agreements. In the months leading up to the fall of Kabul, Afghans who had collaborated with the NATO contingent for twenty long years struggled to understand what exactly the United States had conceded to the enemy, and why. It mattered less that they had been abandoned than finding out what the conditions of their new isolated status were, and the consequences they would have to face. Essentially, they had no way of preparing for or preventing the worst.

In early July 2021, a month and a half before the fall of Kabul, a delegation from the Afghan government traveled to Washington to discuss the transition process, how their collaboration would continue once the withdrawal of troops was completed, and the interim government that would replace them. Both sides resented each other and were fed up with each other's behavior. On July 2, when a journalist asked Joe Biden about the talks with the Afghans and the plans for the withdrawal, the president replied that, with the Fourth of July approaching, he preferred to talk about "happy things."[44] Shaharzad Akbar, part of the delegation and then-president of the Afghanistan Independent Human Rights Commission, later recounted that, after hearing President Biden's comment, she canceled all her appointments, locked herself in her hotel room in Washington, and spent Independence Day crying.[45]

The inefficiency, kleptomania, and conniving manner of the Afghan governments—under both Hamid Karzai and Ashraf Ghani—helped erode American trust. The Doha agreement, meanwhile, which the United States negotiated exclusively with the Taliban, convinced Afghan leadership that not only would the United States no longer support them, but that it would do nothing to prevent the dissolution of the Republic. At his final meeting with Biden's military advisor—prior to the withdrawal—Amrullah Saleh, the former Afghan vice-president and ex-head of the secret service, who did not flee when Kabul fell but stayed and fought, was fast to point out that "Even the weapons we have on our helicopters . . . expire in September 2021."[46]

During the twenty-year war, 3,590 soldiers from the international coalition died, 2,465 of whom were American. In just twelve years (the UN mission that documented Afghan losses started in 2009), at least 70,000 Afghan soldiers died. These numbers simply do not support the theory that Afghans were unwilling to fight for their Republic in August 2021 and, therefore, that this is the reason why Kabul fell.

The Doha agreement laid out the details for the withdrawal of the Americans, including technicians, without whom many weapons left as a legacy to the Afghan Armed Forces were unusable. The Afghans were left with 210 military bases that they could not operate on their own, and dozens of helicopters they could not fly because they were missing instruments that the pilots needed.[47]

When the retreat began, all American helicopters were grounded, making it impossible to bring ammunition, food, and water to Afghan soldiers at the bases near the front. As soon as the first base was abandoned by local soldiers when they ran out of food, the troops in the base nearby started to lose hope, triggering a domino effect. On July 2, the most important US military base in Afghanistan, Bagram, was evacuated. The

Republic had not yet collapsed, but five thousand prisoners, including members of the Taliban and other criminals and terrorists, were freed. Afghan leaders were enraged and interpreted the move as a serious offense with a hostile message: We no longer believe in you.

Saleh had this to say: "If you want to leave, that is totally fine. But don't negotiate with the Taliban and then depart. This leaves us . . . to manage the mess, pain and uncertainty."[48] His people wondered why Washington didn't hand over the prisoners to the Republic instead of setting them free, especially if they expected the Republic to carry on without them.

The Americans left three and a half million items—from cars to night vision goggles—at the Bagram base. The Afghan military was not informed, so when the Americans switched off the lights at three o'clock in the morning and left Bagram, the looters got there first and took everything they could. The Afghans saw this as yet another punishment, an offense, and a clear message.

The Taliban's plan was simple: all we have to do is wait. As the well-known, perhaps inaccurate, and yet realistic Taliban saying goes, "You have the clocks but we have the time." Washington made a public announcement as to when the final soldiers would leave Afghanistan, and never once considered retaining a small unit of 2,500 soldiers for deterrence, as they had in Korea. Nor were they in the least bit vague about the timing and mode of their departure, which would have also given their partners and allies a slight advantage. A small contingent would not have fought to keep the status quo, but it could have assured a safer, more orderly, and more complete evacuation. It would have upheld the terms outlined in the Doha agreement, which were still on the table before the fall of Kabul on August 15: a government that included the Taliban but was not comprised solely of them; a territorial arrangement that allowed for Taliban-controlled provinces as well as enclaves—like Kabul and the Panjshir Valley—where Afghans could continue to live in safety and under the norms that had been implemented in the past twenty years.

The hardline faction always wins

Nangarhar province is two hundred kilometers from Kabul in the far eastern part of Afghanistan; it takes half a day to get there by car, the road winding through gorges and crevasses, one hairpin turn after the next. The provincial capital, Jalalabad, has one hundred fifty thousand inhabitants. Al Qaeda and Islamic State militants in Afghanistan hide in the surrounding mountains. Following the Islamic State attack at Kabul Airport on August 26, 2021, bombs came raining down on the area via American drones, avenging the death of thirteen US soldiers and one hundred seventy Afghans.

This land, which sits on the border with Pakistan, traditionally belongs to the Haqqani clan. In the past, when a Western drone struck the area, it was often assumed, for lack of information, that it had taken out one of the key figures in the terrorist network. These days, the clan's leadership, including Sirajuddin himself, have never been better. They were actually the first to enter Kabul on August 15, which gave them a bargaining chip they used profitably with the Taliban. The purpose of my trip is to gain perspective on the new Minister of the Interior from the land where he has held power for decades.

If you're a Western woman and travelling to Nangarhar, a burka is not a nuisance, it's an advantage. It protects you from women and children who, under the pretext of begging, peer into car windows and report anything out of the ordinary back to the terrorist groups in the mountains. The road bypasses a vast military base that was run solely by the Americans, and not by any of the other coalition countries; this is both the most strategic and the most dangerous location for waging war on terrorism.

In Jalalabad, I was a guest of Ahmad, a former official from the Western-aligned government, who escaped with his wife and children during the evacuation but then returned to try and convince his parents and siblings to leave the country, too, explaining to them that they were in great danger.

My local contact is Rahma, Ahmad's mother. I've been writing to her for days, and it was she who originally invited me into their home. On the day we're supposed to meet, she sends me a message and photo at nine o'clock in the morning, "Look, I've already started cooking for you," and when I arrive, she's been cooking for four hours. She prepared an eight-course lunch, but because of me—because I am accompanied by two men, two strangers who are not part of Rahma's family—she can neither join us nor enjoy the stew, lamb kofta, and Kabuli rice pilaf seasoned with meat, raisins, and sweet carrots. We're not in Kabul but a Taliban stronghold where the women's demonstrations we in the West saw on television in August and September never took place.

While we eat, the men in Ahmad's family tell me what happened in Jalalabad on August 19, 2021, which may well have been the final Afghanistan independence day, their last chance to fly the green, red, and black national flag.

On August 19, Ahmad's brother took to the streets carrying the Afghan flag, which the Taliban hate; they want their flag to be the only one on display. He was with a friend, a literature teacher at the local high school. The teacher had arranged to meet up with all his students in the square. The two men walked through the bazaar together on their way to the celebrations. Ahmad's father told me what happened: "They didn't kill them immediately, shooting randomly into the crowd, because that wouldn't have sent a strong enough message. To punish men like my son, they needed to use crueler methods. Naturally, they fired their guns into the air to disperse the crowd, as they always do, but they're so inept that they accidentally killed some of their own people. Then came the executions. They shot my son in the alley directly behind us, the one you just drove through in your car. We washed away the blood, but the stain is still there. They killed him while he was coming home to us." Others assassinated on that August 19 include a local journalist, a high school employee, his son's teacher friend, and four of the teacher's students who had eagerly come out to demonstrate. A few nights later, a lawyer known to Ahmad's family, who worked for the government in Jalalabad, was dragged out of his house and executed in the street for everyone to see. The act of forcibly removing people from their homes and killing them, instead of shooting them in the chaos of the main square, is to communicate that these deaths are not collateral damage, they're executions.

Haqqani's men, who never pretended they'd respect the Doha agreement, used the same methods they had always used for punishing enemies, infidels, and traitors. The Haqqani clan was founded by Jalaluddin Haqqani in the 1980s, when Afghan Islamists were at war with the Soviets, who in turn were massacring locals with weapons much more powerful than the Afghans. This was the period when the United States regularly sent weapons to the mujahideen resistance, and in particular to the Northern Alliance. The territory where the Haqqani operate, along the border with Pakistan, was both a crucial transit corridor for weapons passing through Pakistan and a strategic access point, the shortest route to the capital.

The television is on during our lunch: Tolo News. During a replay of Secretary of State Antony Blinken's interview with the Afghan network, Ahmad's youngest brother, who is only fourteen, gets to his feet, leaps across the tablecloth spread out on the carpet, and over a homemade air conditioner made from a motorcycle engine, and switches off the television. It's a simple but solemn gesture.

Washington was annoyed: Blinken was criticizing the proposed Taliban government, which was the opposite of inclusive.

Ahmad's teenage brother recalled how his older brother had worked side by side with Americans for twenty years, how they had promised him that he'd be safe after they left, that no one would touch him. And instead, he was executed before the Americans even left Afghanistan.

The person responsible for shutting down protests and minority uprisings after the allied withdrawal was the new Minister of the Interior, Sirajuddin. He was in charge of searching the homes of Afghan civilians suspected of collaborating with the West, and he was the one who signed off on executions. The Haqqani clan is the hardline faction of the Taliban, as well as the increasingly dominant one. Younger and more brutal than the older generation, they are gradually sidelining the "moderate" wing that, technically speaking, led the armed movement to victory by signing the Doha agreements with the Trump administration, which laid out the complete withdrawal of foreign soldiers. The promises made with that agreement were not very credible and have not been maintained. It's hard to say if this is because the "moderate" faction never really intended to respect the agreement, or because it could not—because the hardline faction exerted more power.

A longstanding rivalry exists between the Haqqani clan and Mullah Baradar—the co-founder of the Taliban movement, deputy prime minister of the new government, and above all, the man who negotiated the peace agreements in Doha. The clash between his faction and the Haqqani clan reached a critical point in 2007 that saw the clan's exit from the Supreme Council, the Shura of Quetta. Baradar's recent actions have been more pragmatic, but Haqqani's extremism is paying off in terms of power. Its network oversees the security apparatus and trains special forces, such as the Badri 313 brigade, deployed in strategic hubs in Kabul—such as the international airport—and in the fight against the Islamic State. Haqqani men even stand outside the large military base on the road to Jalalabad, the one that used to belong to the Americans. If security and territorial control are what the Taliban need for legitimacy, Haqqani forces have already attained an indispensable position. They are essentially untouchable.

The eastern territories dominated by Haqqani are strategically important and a key to their ascent in power. A number of gangs of the Islamic State, the Taliban's main internal enemy, began to relocate here when, in 2017, things started to go wrong for the group that heads them—the Islamic State of Iraq and Syria.

The first to arrive in Afghanistan were the women. The ISIS wives crossed the border carrying heaps of money that had to be protected from advancing local armies and bombings by the international coalition. They knew they had to hurry, that the caliphate would one day need those funds. They did not need to be reminded that they were expendable and replaceable. Their husbands (or their jailers, as the case may be), the ones who survived, joined them later; they now live in the mountains and in rural villages. They live in the gorges around Jalalabad, as did members of Al Qaeda, which was founded by Osama bin Laden in Peshawar, Pakistan, less than two hours' drive from here. Over time, the Islamic State has become the chief instigator of terror, surpassing even Al Qaeda. Now, Al Qaeda prefers illegal trafficking and trade over martyrdom and suicide attacks.

In Nangarhar, a long-standing and privileged relationship with the Haqqani network grants Al Qaeda almost total freedom of action. The Islamic State, meanwhile, in its search for theological and political purity, can consider itself a hardline organization, proud that it has never buckled to compromises. The Islamic State uses Al Qaeda's lack of initiative and the Taliban's new role as a "diplomatic force" to recruit new potential martyrs.

With every change in power comes winners and losers, insiders and outsiders, opportunists and outcasts. The Islamic

State has enrolled many disillusioned ex-Taliban members and will continue to do so.

One of the women who carried money belonging to the Islamic State into Afghanistan in 2017 is a young Uzbek woman who lived for eight years in Nangarhar among men and women of the group. Harvard researcher Vera Mironova—an expert on Islamic terrorism and, in particular, on women in the Islamic State—met the young woman in a recovery program for radicalized people in Uzbekistan, to which she has belonged since the summer of 2019. She was the first person to speak openly about the new "global village" of terrorists that the Islamic State has created in Afghanistan. In Nangarhar, she lived alongside many other foreigners: French, German, Canadian, Russian, and Chinese Uyghurs who had recently arrived from the Xinjiang region, a small strip of land in north-eastern Afghanistan.

The way she described it, the network is organized into families with children, either real or fictitious, arranged to blend in better with the local population, so as not to appear suspicious. Afghan, Tajik, and Uzbek fighters are in charge, as they're the ones who know the region best and have the most experience in the field. They oversee training, plan recruitment propaganda, and decide on operations, such as the one in the spring of 2021, during which a suicide bomber blew himself up at the funeral of a local police commander in Nangarhar, killing twenty-five people lined up to say their final prayers in front of the body. Or like the bombing of the maternity ward in the Kabul hospital, in the Hazara district with its Shiite majority, with beds for a hundred newborns and run by Doctors Without Borders, during which sixteen people died.

In 2023, it was discovered that the Islamic State was recruiting members in Europe via Telegram, focusing on young, second or third generation German Muslims; the same technique was used in the glory years of the Islamic State of Iraq and the Levant, which led to more recent attacks in Europe.

Burka Avengers

The burka is a pre-Islamic garment dating back to the 15th century. Originally, it was black—today in Afghanistan, it is mainly blue—and it was designed to save women. Actually, it was introduced to make life better for men, but a side effect was that it saved the lives of adulteresses, or women suspected of infidelity. Prior to its invention, the punishment for women guilty of adultery was death, but this led to the presence of too many orphans in the street—who needed care and who bothered men with their begging and tantrums. To solve this problem, men decided to cover women from head to toe, isolate them from society, and make them all but disappear, alive only to care for young children.

When I was in Afghanistan, at night I would watch Tolo TV, a channel that belongs to the network that aired the news at Ahmad's house, but that broadcasts much more than news. The quality of Tolo's programs is high, and I particularly enjoyed an animated series called *Burka Avenger*. It was well written, engaging, with technically impressive animation.

The protagonist is Jiya, a teacher in a girls' school who wears a light hijab in the classroom, and an avenger of wrongs who dons a dark burka when she's on a mission. Actually, it's as if the burka grants her a superpower: she can move around incognito, undisturbed, and invisible until she needs to strike. Her one goal is to fight the bad guys who want to shut down the school. The principal villain is a corrupt local politician who bears an uncanny resemblance to a stylized figure of a Taliban soldier. Generally speaking, the references to reality in Afghanistan are far from subtle. The stories are smart, with numerous ironic and surreal elements. *Burka Avenger* is not just an animated series for children, but something akin to *The Simpsons* or *South Park*, with a powerful subtext for adults. It promotes education for girls in a clever way, combining the burka with emancipation, portraying the article of clothing not as an impediment but as a harmless, even useful, tool. The authors are trying to be inclusive, in that they don't want to divide a society that includes adult women who cover themselves completely; they've found a way of successfully insinuating into traditionalist households and speaking to the girls of the family. They challenge norms without appearing like a threat—just like the show's protagonist.

Even in Nangarhar, the most conservative province of Afghanistan, *Burka Avenger* had numerous female viewers. Ahmad's mother told me that "it played an important part in making education for girls an important and shared value."

From my hotel room, I wondered what would eventually happen to *Burka Avenger* and the rest of the programs on Tolo TV under the Taliban. After the fall of Kabul, the media company did not declare war outright on the regime, but protested by continuing to broadcast programs that were popular, employing women in the entertainment and information industry, and providing news. For Tolo TV, resistance means not panicking but carrying on in a professional manner, without change—whether that means continuing to broadcast an investigative report or a cartoon series.

When, in May 2022, the Taliban law came into effect that required women to cover their faces in public, Tolo News's male commentators responded by appearing with their own faces covered. They weren't breaking any rules, they were making a statement. On the day that female news anchors had to choose between wearing a burka or losing their job, their male colleagues stood by them so they didn't have to make that humiliating choice in silence, thereby sending a powerful message into the homes of millions of Afghans.

Although the edict does not refer specifically to burkas, it forces women to cover their faces, eyes excluded. The cloth has to be loose enough to render the features of their bodies unrecognizable, and consequently of a dark and relatively thick fabric, as a thin material would adhere to the person's shape as they moved. The rules were decided by the Ministry for the Propagation of Virtue and the Repression of Vice. In fact, one of the first things the Taliban did when they came to power was convert the Ministry for the Inclusion of Women of the Afghan Republic—a version of an Equal Opportunities office—into an institution that pursues the exact opposite objectives.

Tolo TV has another problem: it broadcasts many foreign television series. Its most watched programs include melodramatic and highly popular Turkish soap operas, where female figures are not covered head to toe. Tolo's programming is also varied: they broadcast quiz shows and reality shows, where teams face off against each other in individual or group challenges, including athletic ones. Slowly, women are disappearing from these shows because they refuse to take part in burkas.

After the Taliban's return, Tolo News continued to broadcast the news. They reported on the execution of members of the old regime, including Ahmad's brother in Nangarhar. They reported on how educator Ismail Mashal was tortured for appearing on television and saying that he would never stop distributing books to girls, that doing so went against his principles as an educator. Tolo News made the public aware of the arrest of Matiullah Wesa for similar reasons.

The network adopts a simple trick. The titles and leads include comments like: "The government declares false the news that . . . " or "The government denies that . . . " This ploy allows them to delve into the stories, explaining them in online articles or broadcasting investigative reports that recount events the Taliban doesn't like to acknowledge, but which are true. One such story has to do with the vast numbers of people who are fleeing Afghanistan because of the humanitarian disaster, which the Taliban has no idea how to even begin to resolve. Tolo News has also given ample airtime to another critical issue: namely, the Taliban are understaffed.

Their men know how to do only one thing—fight. While the schools in Nangarhar have gradually emptied out of girls, they have filled up with male adults who show up in class with rifles slung over their shoulders: twenty-year-old members of the Haqqani clan who cannot read, write, or do basic math. It's impossible to examine documents at checkpoints in high-risk areas, where Islamic State incursions are a daily occurrence, if you cannot read.

The Taliban men don't know how to do maintenance on bridges, run a central bank, manage the health system, oversee sewers and railways and dams, or monitor seismicity in schools or mines. The Afghans with these skills—engineers, nurses, economists, and so on—have no intention of working for the Taliban, and have been the first to flee. These people have a greater chance of building a future abroad than a local farmer or animal breeder does. The desire to leave the country has struck the most valuable members of a generation; the best educated are those who are also the most traumatized by the fundamentalists' return to power.

Twenty years cannot be erased

Omar is twenty-seven years old, slender, and wears his longish hair tied back in a ponytail. Zahra is twenty-four; she has dark eyes, a dazzling smile, and wears a floral veil, preferring jeans to long skirts. Omar and Zahra are married. They're journalists and live in the Afghan province of Kapisa, to the northeast of Kabul. Both would like to leave the country. In Kapisa, farmers have stopped laying out their watermelons and grapes in the market stalls because no one has money to buy them. Precious vegetables are for foreigners only; the Taliban buy fruit from local farmers and export it to Pakistan; the remaining potatoes, zucchini, and onions are for the inhabitants of Kapisa. Relying on their intellectual labor, Omar and Zahra earn about a hundred dollars a month each, in a country where the mines are now filled with child laborers. They're almost rich. Almost lucky.

One hundred dollars a month is the average monthly salary of a reporter in Afghanistan—a job none of us would do for a hundred thousand dollars. In May, the Taliban made a second visit to their house, threatened them both, and beat Omar. He and Zahra were so frightened that the following day, they decided to escape and set off across the border into Pakistan.

Living in Pakistan as refugees, without work and with the meager savings that they were able to put aside, they did not last long. Two months later, Zahra and Omar crossed back over the border and returned to Kapisa. They had wasted energy and money on a desperate and pointless journey. At that point, they were poor even by Afghan standards.

The terrifying, courageous, and unforgettable evacuations from Hamid Karzai International Airport in Kabul saved some 100,000 Afghans. American flights carried 82,000 to safety, the British saved 9,000, the Italian operation Aquila Omnia evacuated 4,890 civilians, Germany saved 4,200, and France about 2,000. One hundred thousand is a vast number of people considering the conditions, but insignificant with regards to how many Afghan men and women needed—and still need—to escape.

As Zahra said, "The foreigners who came here at the beginning of the millennium owed something to all the people who aided them, who numbered in the hundreds of thousands, and not all of them were taken to safety. But what about the teenage girls of Kapisa, for whom going to school became the norm; don't they deserve their help, too? The illusion of protection has claimed many victims, and not just in an abstract sense. Think of the women who got divorced from violent husbands, men who now feel as though they have the right to take their wives back, and can't wait to punish them. Don't the foreigners who brought about change owe something to those women, too? If the answer is yes, then the number of people who deserve to leave Afghanistan is actually in the millions."

Omar considered applying for a US humanitarian visa. He had followed the war as a reporter embedded with NATO troops, and showed me his reportages from the front. "I worked with the Americans, and now the Taliban threaten me; that should be enough, right?" But Omar gave up on the visa process before even starting it. The outcome is often disappointing, and the costs are high. Technically, the process is known as a Form I-131, and it costs 575 dollars per person just to start the paperwork. That means 1,150 USD for the two of them, a year's salary for Omar, who no longer has a job. "If I thought for a minute that there was a chance of success, I'd find a way of coming up with the money. But it's clear that the system is designed to discourage people from trying, and almost impossible to succeed." By the end of summer 2022, a year after the fall of Kabul, the US government had approved only 0.2% of 66,000 visa applications that had been completed and paid for by Afghan citizens. Although that number might seem high, it's actually very low; the $575 application fee is prohibitively high in Afghanistan. Of those 66,000 visa applications, the United States processed fewer than 8,000 and approved only 123.[49]

Zahra has no recollection of the old regime. In 2001, she was four years old. She has worn a brightly colored hijab her whole life, but has never had to cover her face. Since completing her studies, she's worked as a journalist and TV news anchor. Her whole life was built on the one premise that those terrible five years, or so, when the Taliban were in power, which she heard about from her parents and grandparents, were a thing of the past.

She never believed any of the false promises made by spokesman Zabiullah Mujahid after the conquest of Kabul, but she knows that Afghan society is no longer the same as it was in the 1990s, and that the Taliban was gone for long enough for new habits to take root. "There are simply too many of us. In areas where people don't accept the regime, they'd need an official in every building and at every intersection to enforce all the rules they impose on us."

In Kabul, in Herat to the west, and in the northern city of Mazar-i-Sharif, some women still drive, wear high-heeled shoes, and disobey the rule of covering their faces in public. There are grey zones. There are endless acts of rebellion that don't make headlines but do change lives. There are girls' schools that have stayed open despite the bans. There are teachers who continue to teach online in secret. There are fake Koranic schools where the students read math books instead of the Koran. There are brothers who listen carefully in class and then come home and share their notes with their sisters. There are mothers who cut their daughters' hair extremely short and dress them like boys so they can go to school. "Families who take risks so that their daughters can continue going to school are everywhere—in northern Afghanistan and Kabul, they're the norm," Zahra says. Since leaving her job as a television show host, she homeschools teenage girls who are no longer allowed to attend high school.

Women who studied to be doctors, but who were prevented from graduating, treat patients in secret and help other women give birth at home. They want to save lives and prevent the childbirth mortality rates from returning to the catastrophic figures of 2001. They want to give meaning to their years of hard work, of studying anatomy; they want to follow their ambitions. Young men marry their female friends just to help them out, because you can hardly do anything without a husband, you can't even travel more than seventy kilometers from home. In fictitious unions such as these, fake husbands don't expect sex, clean laundry, or meals on the table. "People had hopes, learned skills, nurtured dreams, and set things in motion. Now they're adapting in order to survive," Omar says. Seeing Afghan women and girls, who have far more troubles than their Iranian counterparts, find the strength to protest in Kabul and Herat in solidarity with the *Jin, Jiyan, Azadi* movement that broke out after the death of Mahsa Amini in Tehran, was unthinkable, and yet it happened.

When I interviewed Mayor Zarifa Ghafari, I asked her what, if anything, simply can't be erased after twenty years of life in Afghanistan without the Taliban. I asked her how many other fathers there are today like hers, who wish for daughters, in the hopes of raising them in freedom.

"There are many fathers like mine. You have no idea just how many parents take risks so that their daughters can continue to study. The solidarity that exists between men and women within our families, and within couples generally, cannot be erased merely by the withdrawal of foreign troops."

It would be a huge miscalculation to consider twenty years of life without the Taliban as pointless or a waste. A large segment of Afghanistan will never go back, or give up; people will not conform to the regime, except in minimal and performative ways. Many Afghans today look on the Taliban as a movement that has been around for less time than mobile phones, as a movement that has controlled only parts of the country—and never completely—for only seven non-consecutive years.

For many Afghans, this constitutes a temporary aberration, not their destiny.

Endnotes

I. Being Twenty in Tehran

[1]Some of the names and places have been changed to protect the people in the story.

[2] The Basij, officially known as *Nirouy-e moqavemat-e basij*, is an Iranian paramilitary group created to resist the Iraqi invasion (1980-1988). Since being demobilized at the end of the war, it has been used mainly for internal repression.

[3] In 2023, inflation reached 53%, after years of being at 40%.

[4] "Bassidji" is a documentary made in 2009 by Mehran Tamadon.

[5] Narges Bajoghli, *Iran Reframed: Anxieties of Power in the Islamic Republic*, Stanford: Stanford University Press, 2019.

[6] This is a reference to the heir of the Shah, Reza Pahlavi, and to MEK, the national liberation army.

[7] Matt Burgess, "Iran Built a Facial Recognition System to Identify and Punish Women Who Don't Wear Hijabs," *Wired*, April 5, 2023.

[8] Feranak Amidi, "'Your Car Will Be Confiscated': Iran Women Defy Hijab Law Despite Threats," *BBC News*, June 11, 2023, https://www.bbc.com/news/world-middle-east-65842130.

[9] Cecilia Sala, "In Iran cambia il sistema di controllo delle ragazze: meno poliziotti e più tecnologia. La protesta si trasforma," *Il Foglio*, April 20, 2023.

II. The Ayatollahs

[10] Iran International Newsroom, "Prominent Cleric, Other Insiders Criticize Regime Amid Iran Crises," *Iran International*, April 17, 2023.

[11] Farnaz Fassihi, "Protests Erupt in Iranian Cities After Woman's Death in Custody," *The New York Times*, September 20, 2022.

[12] Mehran Tamadonfar, "Islam, Law, and Political Control in Contemporary Iran," *Journal for the Scientific Study of Religion*, vol. 40, n. 2, June 2001.

[13] Mehran Kamrava, *Triumph and Despair: In Search of Iran's Islamic Republic*, London: Hurst, 2022.

[14] Maziar Motamedi, "Iran's Khamenei Blames Israel, US in First Comments on Protests," *Al Jazeera*, October 3, 2022.

[15] Shadi Hamid, "The Right to Choose to Wear (or Not) Hijab," *Brookings Institution*, January 19, 2016, https://www.brookings.edu/articles/the-right-to-choose-to-wear-or-not-hijab/.

[16] Alex Vatanka, "What the Hijab Protests Mean for Iran's Clerical Class," *Foreign Policy*, September 23, 2022.

[17] Hooman Majd, *The Ayatollah Begs to Differ: The Paradox of Modern Iran*, New York: Doubleday, 2008.

[18] This definition of "Taqiyya" is by the Grand Ayatollah Muḥammad Fazel Lankarani of Qom.

[19] In 2008, the authorities admitted that close to five million satellite dishes existed, allowing people to get through state-run propaganda. Considering that the authorities generally tended to deny the phenomenon altogether, or at least play it down, there were probably many more than that (Asr Iran, November 24, 2008).

[20] The Farsi1 channel shut down in 2016.

[21] Bajoghli, *Iran Reframed.*

[22] Members of the communist party Tudeh and members of the MEK (Mojahedin-e Khalq), historically mixed Islamism and Marxism, while today they stand by a social-democratic manifesto. Both parties are currently banned in Iran.

III. The First Generation

[23] Paola Peduzzi, "La visita di Zelensky sul fronte della guerra a Bakhmut è straordinaria," *Il Foglio*, December 20, 2022.

[24] Paul Sonne, Isabelle Khurshudyan, Serhiy Morgunov, and Kostiantyn Khudov, "Battle for Kyiv: Ukrainian Valor, Russian Blunders Combined to Save the Capital," *Washington Post*, August 24, 2022.

[25] Brett Forrest, "Russian Spy or Ukrainian Hero? The Strange Death of Denys Kiryeyev," *The Wall Street Journal*, January 18, 2023.

[26] Ibid.

[27] Julia Davis, "Morality Shouldn't Get in the Way: Russia's Genocidal State Media," *Center for European Policy Analysis*, March 13, 2023.

[28] Vladimir Putin, *Speech to the Federal Assembly*, February 21, 2023, http://www.en.kremlin.ru/events/president/transcripts/70565.

IV. Putin's Mistake

[29] Lori Hinnant, Mstyslav Chernov and Vasilisa Stepanenko, "AP Evidence Points to 600 Dead in Mariupol Theatre Airstrike," *Associated Press*, May 4, 2022.

[30] Oksana Grytsenko, "'I'm Not a Loser': Zelensky Clashes with Veterans Over Donbas Disengagement," *Kyiv Post*, October 28, 2019.

[31] Susan B. Glasser and Peter Baker, "U.S. Intelligence Opens Its Playbook to Warn of Russian Invasion," *The New York Times*, February 12, 2022.

[32] Anna Politkovskaya, *Putin's Russia*, trans. Arch Tait, London: Harvill Press, 2004.

[33] Similar accounts have been reported by the independent outlet Astra and the X account @wartranslated, which regularly translate and disseminate video testimonies from Russian conscripts and their families.

[34] Chris O-wiki (@ChrisO_wiki), "They made a video outside the prosecutor's office in Voronezh . . .," *X* (formerly *Twitter*), November 11, 2022, https://x.com/ChrisO_wiki/status/1591010385448275968.

[35] Anna Politkovskaya, "La maledizione della Cecenia," *Internazionale*, September 9, 2004.

V. Ghosts

[36] Cecilia Sala, "Zarifa Ghafari ci racconta la battaglia dei padri per far studiare in segreto le loro figlie in Afghanistan," *Il Foglio*, March 11, 2023.

[37] Morgan Ome, "Pelosi, 'Make No Mistake: This Is the Biden Agenda': A Conversation with Speaker of the House, Nancy Pelosi," *The Atlantic*, September 29, 2021.

[38] Joseph R. Biden, Jr., *Remarks by President Biden on Afghanistan*, The White House, August 16, 2021.

[39] Ibid.

[40] David Kilcullen and Greg Mills, *The Ledger: Accounting for Failure in Afghanistan*, London: Hurst, 2021.

[41] Tom O'Connor, "Seeking World Recognition, Taliban Vows to Help Fight Terror and Climate Change," *Newsweek*, August 23, 2021.

[42] John Lloyd, "Bitter Lessons from Afghanistan," *Quillette*, September 22, 2021.

[43] Rory Stewart and Gerald Knaus, *Can Intervention Work?* New York: W.W. Norton, 2011.

[44] Emma Graham-Harrison and Peter Beaumont, "Afghan Anger Over US's Sudden, Silent Bagram Departure," *The Guardian*, July 6, 2021.

[45] Steve Coll, "The Secret History of the U.S. Diplomatic Failure in Afghanistan." *The New Yorker*, December 20, 2021.

[46] Kilcullen and Mills, *The Ledger*, p. 43.

[47] Ibid., p. 32.

[48] Ibid., p. 44.

[49] Najib Aminy and Dhruv Mehrotra, "The US Has Approved Only 123 Afghan Humanitarian Parole Applications in the Last Year," *Reveal*, August 19, 2022.